DRAWING MADE EASY 2
PEOPLE

Felix Lorenzi

Bay Books
Sydney and London

The *Drawing Made Easy* series

Volume 1, Animals
Volume 2, People
Volume 3, Perspective
Volume 4, Nature

This edition published by Bay Books
61–69 Anzac Parade
Kensington, NSW 2033
Publisher: George Barber
ISBN 0 85835 760 7

BBR 89
Printed in Singapore

Preface

Anyone capable of drawing his impressions and experiences will tell you that he not only develops his creativity and finds great enjoyment in doing so, but he also learns more about his surroundings. This applies to everyone — child, teenager and adult — who wants to try drawing and is looking for some way of learning how.

This book, the second volume of the *Drawing Made Easy* series, concentrates on the human body. It breaks down and simplifies all the basic forms; in such a way a fuller understanding of the nature of the human body is achieved. Using this method, both children and adults can learn the 'secrets' of drawing objects and gain a greater awareness of the nature of shapes and proportions. Once the basics outlined in this book have been mastered, more complex drawing skills and, finally, the ability to draw freely will be well within reach. Once again, the drawing school is above all a school for observation.

First of all, the human body is broken down into simple geometric shapes and proportions. Only after this has been done can hands, feet, the nose, the mouth and the eyes be drawn. Later, clothes, movement and expression can be added. So, by first simplifying things, it is then possible to proceed to the finer points of free drawing.

But it is not always personal things that the aspiring artist seeks to draw. Often there will be things to draw from daily life, school or work that at first glance seem far too difficult.

What this book is endeavouring to do is to give the beginner, or the person still unsure of himself, help which, within a given framework, will enable him to draw with some success. And perhaps some of you will discover talents of which you were completely unaware or which you thought were not good enough.

The method is structured in such a way that exercises are presented step by step. Whether you are young or old, you will soon find enjoyment in your own efforts and progress.

Instructions

Drawing people, with all their movements, facial expressions and gestures, the right size and build, is often an overwhelming task. Just how and where do you begin?

The best way to start is to break down the body into its individual parts by using a model. Only when you can see clearly the individual parts of the body and their relative proportions will you be able to draw people properly. So, first of all you must learn to see things in their simplified forms. Once you have grasped the relationship between the various parts of the body you can begin sketching them.

The method proposed here — the breaking down of the body into separate parts — will provide for anyone willing to learn the means of drawing successfully.

How does the artist see people?

Put simply, a person is a tall figure standing upright on two feet. Each part of the body exists in a specific relationship with the other parts.

The best drawing aid to use is a type of graph. It helps to establish everything as part of a basic model. Each part of the body can be drawn and then added on in the correct proportions.

Firstly, have a close look at the human body. It stands on two feet with the legs next to each other and the arms hanging down by each side. It is motionless. When the body is in this position the relative proportions of the different parts are easily seen. Try it out yourself by standing thus. You will notice that, for example, your elbows are on about the same vertical level as your hands or that your hands, when stretched out, reach down to your thighs. Observations like this are important.

Start with simple shapes!

Just as with the animals in Volume 1, it is necessary to find suitable basic geometric shapes in order to produce two-dimensional drawings of the human body: the head is simplified to form an ellipse, and the neck forms a rectangle. The chest, arms and legs all become long rectangles; the hands and feet become smaller rectangles.

This is the human body in its simplified form. But, to really grasp this basic model, it helps to first mould it out of clay or plasticine. The three-dimensional model gives us a concrete idea of what we are going to draw.

Now look at the body part by part to see how it is possible to break it down. Start with the head. Firstly, divide the body into 'lengths'. The head of a normal person equals one length of his total height. Draw an axis through the length of the body, dividing it into a right side and a left side. Along this axis, draw eight intervals, each the length of the head. The chest is made up of two of these intervals and the middle of the body occurs at the fourth interval, which is equivalent to the lower edge of the abdomen, where the legs join the body.

A graph placed over the body can also help with the continuation of the drawing: it becomes easier to add the other parts. The knees occur at the sixth interval. The outstretched hand ends half-way down the thigh and the elbows are situated just above the third interval. These same markers are also useful when the various parts of the body are in motion and in different positions — movement will be discussed later.

It is possible to draw this structure from different angles: from the front and the side. Notice how the body is much narrower from the side than from the front. Practise often so that you become familiar with the correct proportions. Then you will be ready for the next stage.

The next stage involves drawing a three-dimensional picture of a person. Once more, a graph is used, but this time it is a three-dimensional graph. This is how you find your reference points. Instead of basic geometric shapes, you can now use rounded ones. Two-dimensional shapes turn into three-dimensional bodies. Notice the slightly sloping shoulder-line and the way the upper surfaces of the feet become visible.

For the next step, use the same structure but add more detail, so that the human body gradually takes form. The shoulder joints and knees are clearly drawn as circles, muscles are added to the thighs, and the feet become small triangles. In this way the joints, which will later be vital for movement, become apparent. The body can be drawn in this way from the front, and from the side as well. The differences between the side and the front views become very clear: the chest and buttock muscles bulge out in the side view. Three-dimensional drawing requires a great deal of practice.

The visible differences between man, woman and child

There are certain differences between the bodies of men, women and children. A woman is normally a bit smaller than a man, and a child smaller than a woman. One of the typical features of a man's body is his wide chest: the width of the chest generally equals that of the hips, and the muscles are more developed. As with the basic model, the male body is divided into eight intervals, each the length of the head.

One of the important distinguishing features of the outline of a woman's body is that the hips are generally noticeably wider than the shoulders. The proportions (eight intervals, each the length of the head) remain unchanged but the woman has a smaller build. As in the basic model, the lower edge of the abdomen forms the middle of the body. The knees are at the sixth interval and the tips of the fingers at the fifth.

Compare a ten-year-old child with a three-year-old. Considerable differences in their relative proportions become obvious. For the ten-year-old child seven intervals are necessary. The middle of the body is then between the third and fourth interval. Other features remain unchanged: the hands reach half-way down the thighs and the knees are situated just below the fifth interval.

With the three-year-old child there are greater differences in the proportions. The length of the whole body is only five times that of the head. The navel is situated in the middle and the lower edge of the abdomen is further down, at the third interval. The knees are at the fourth and the tips of the fingers reach down about this far as well.

A graph is also used for these drawings. In this way it is easy to see how the width of the body changes in relation to the length.

Why an eight-part model?

A basic model is necessary in order to draw a simplified picture. Of course, every person is built differently and this means that the dimensions used are averages only. Every person varies in some way from these averages, and it is through these variations that individual characteristics arise. The basic model provides a means of seeing the ways in which people differ.

But how do you change this model to draw different builds? If, for instance, nine 'head lengths' instead of eight are used, a very tall, thin person will be the result. And, similarly, if only seven 'head lengths' are used, a stocky, fat person is the result. Go back to the graph and compare the variations in individual dimensions.

Besides fat and thin people, people with other builds can also be drawn merely by altering the eight-part model. Once you have thoroughly practised drawing the model in all its variations you can become more flexible in your drawing. And, in fact, to really be able to draw with complete flexibility and ease, you should eventually forget the basic model altogether.

People only come to life through movement

If the axis of the body is moved in some way a drawing immediately gains movement. On page 19 you can see how changing the legs (standing leg and free leg) alters the way the figure stands. The whole body weight rests solely on the standing leg while the free leg serves to prop up the body. This movement results in a shifting of the body weight from one side of the axis to the other.

With walking and running the shifting of body weight is even more apparent. And remember the arms. If you watch closely you will see that they also move when a person is walking — but they move in the opposite direction to the legs: when the right arm is swung forward, the right leg is back. This prevents the body from swaying.

Observe the world with open eyes!

If you want to draw people properly, you must observe them constantly. How does a person sit or lie? How does he move his body when doing different activities? What does his face look like when he is laughing, or when he is angry? If you observe carefully the things around you, your drawings will become more life-like and expressive.

Look around for ideas. Always have a sketchbook with you. Capture your observations with pencil and paper! Once you have had some practice, your drawing will teach you to look at things more closely. And learning to look more closely will in turn improve your drawing.

And, hopefully, you will have great fun learning to draw. Just proceed step by step, following the instructions that accompany the explanatory sketches.

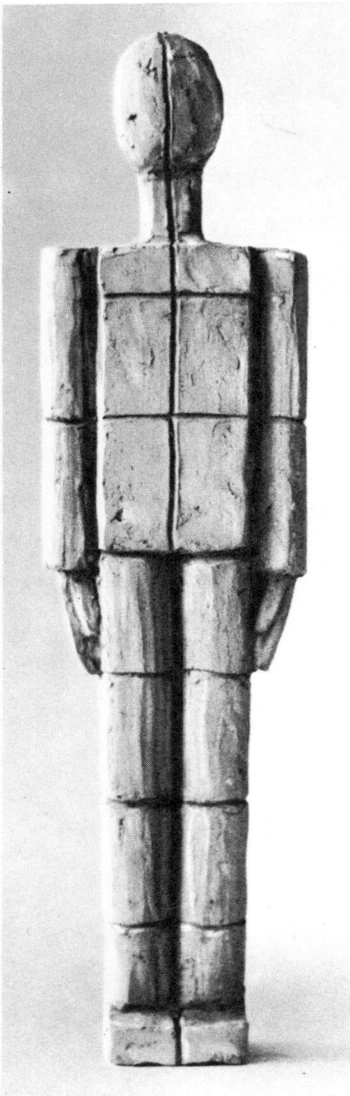

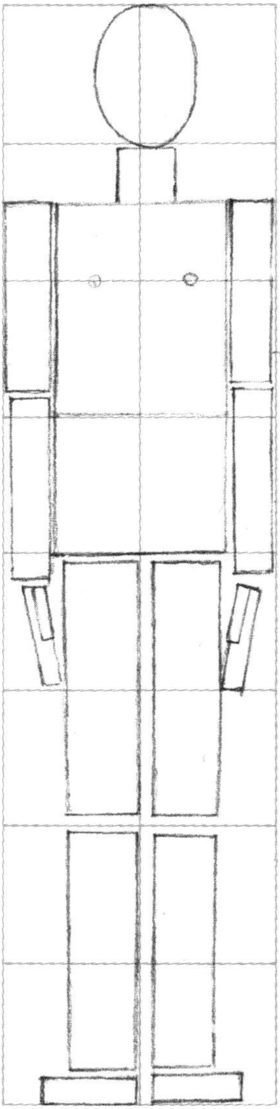

Method one

A very simple figure is modelled from clay or plasticine. The head is the shape of an egg, the torso is like a cube, the arms and legs are long cylinders, and for the feet and hands you can model small tiles.

Now you can do the same thing on paper. The head becomes an ellipse, the upper part of the body a rectangle, and the arms and legs long rectangles.

A coloured graph clarifies the breakdown of the figure into individual parts. The central vertical line, the body's axis, divides the figure in half and will become very important later when movement is studied.

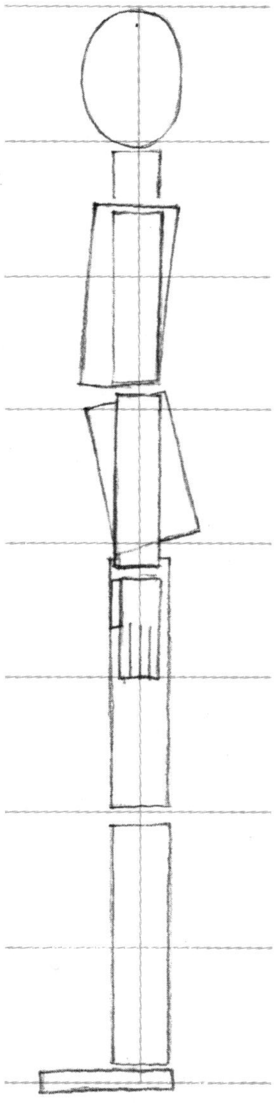

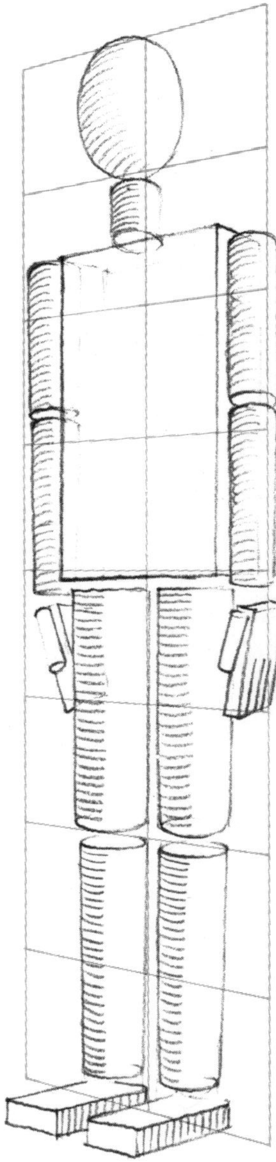

Now a side view: the upper part of the body is narrower, the hands are wider, and the length of the feet can be seen clearly. However, the number of 'head-lengths' remains the same.

A half-profile: the two-dimensional shapes can be seen and drawn in three dimensions. The torso looks like a long box and the arms and legs resemble cylinders. Try to find other angles.

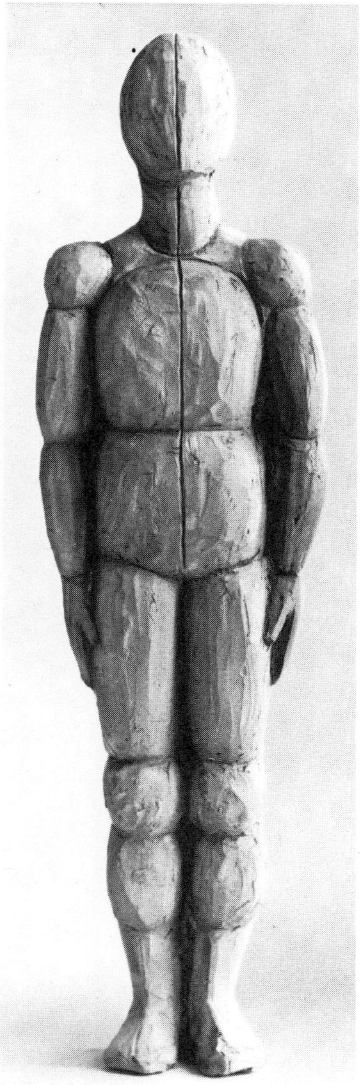

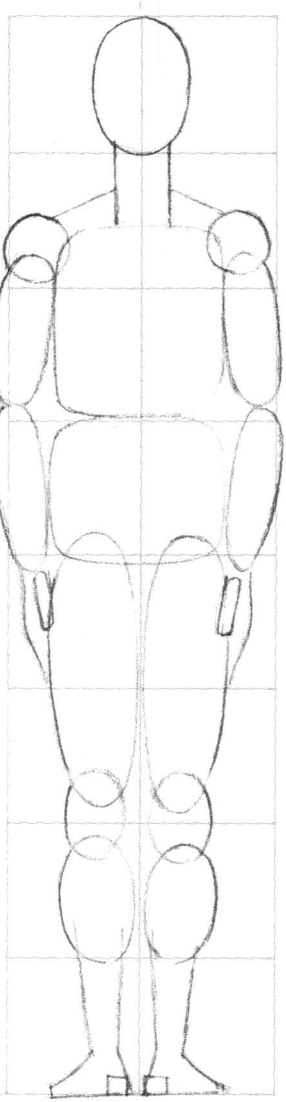

Method two

This figure looks more life-like because it is rounded. The abdomen is seen more clearly, and the shoulders and knees are accentuated by small, rounded shapes. The thigh muscles are also accentuated by rounding off the figure.

Go back to the drawing. The head is still an ellipse but the shoulder joints have now become circles. The abdomen is a rounded-off rectangle, the thighs are long ellipses, and so on. In spite of this, the proportions remain the same.

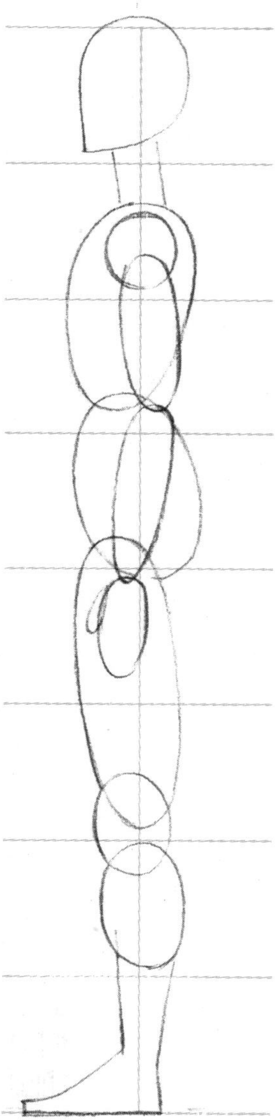

In the side view the shapes are rounded off as well. Notice how the knees and the buttock muscles have become more pronounced.

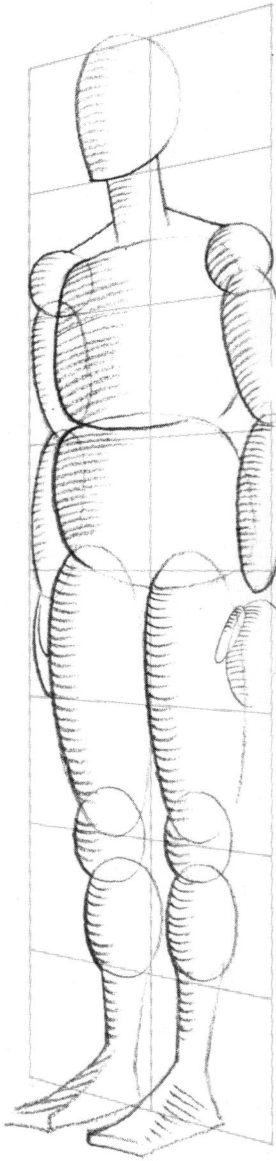

For a three-dimensional picture, turn the figure round again into a semi-profile position. Add some shading to accentuate particular parts of the body. To do this, you must first decide where the light is coming from.

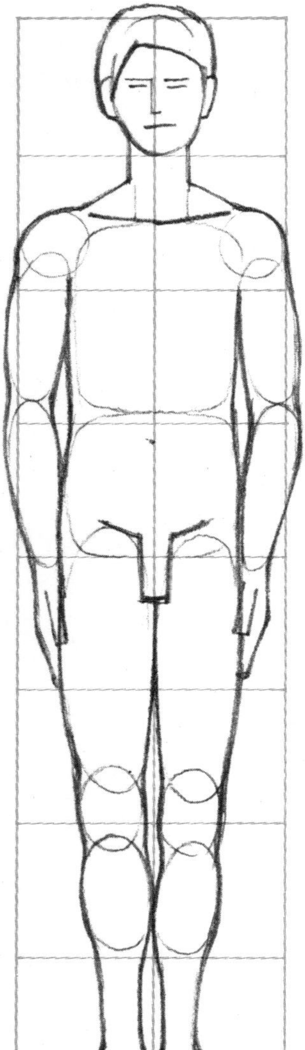

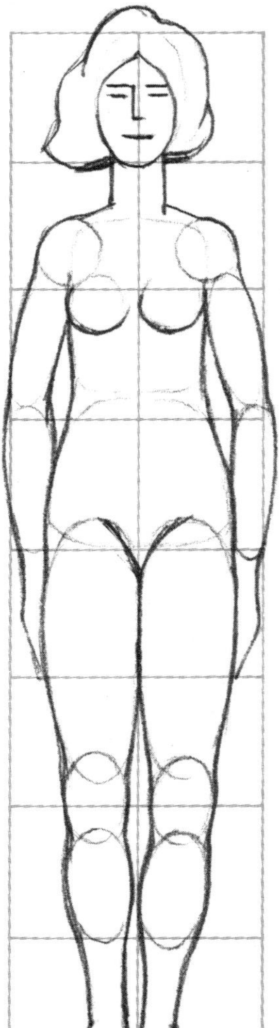

The differences between men, women and children

A man's build corresponds to the proportions of the basic model. His muscular system is more developed and he is taller than a woman. His chest is about as wide as his hips.

In comparison to a man, a woman has a slighter build. The upper part of her body is narrower, but her hips are wider. However, although she is smaller, the number of 'head-lengths' remains the same. And her hands also reach down to about the middle of her thighs.

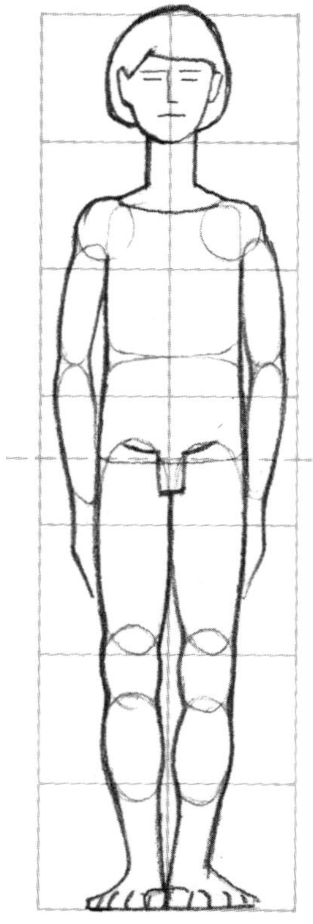

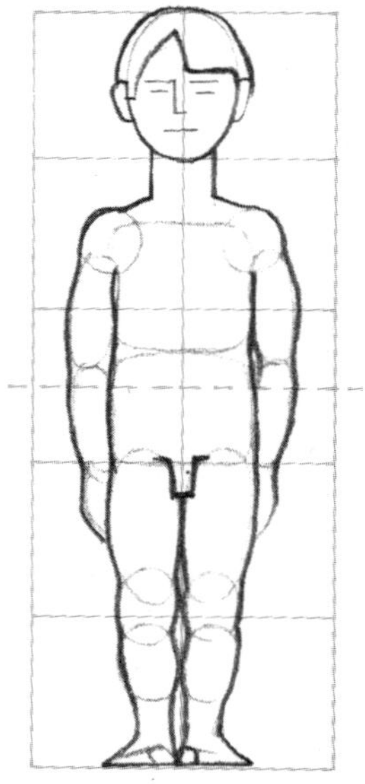

For a ten-year-old child the number of 'head-lengths' is reduced to seven. The outstretched arms extend half-way down the thighs.

There are even greater variations in the proportions of a three-year-old child. His body is five times the length of his head. The middle of his body is the navel, so that his body appears to be more rounded.

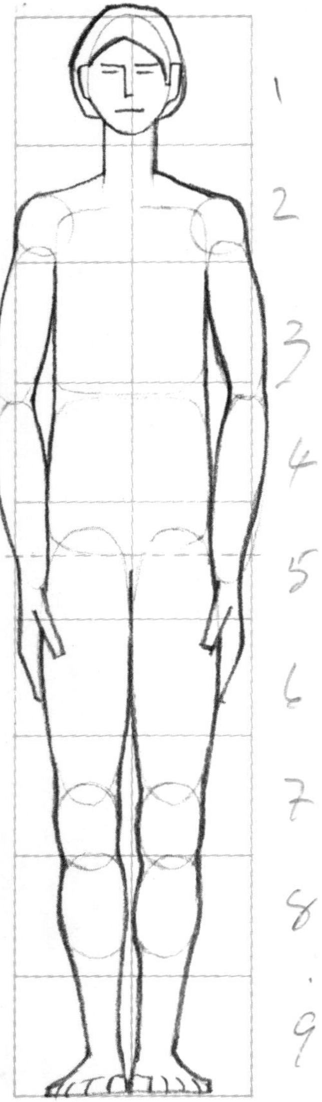

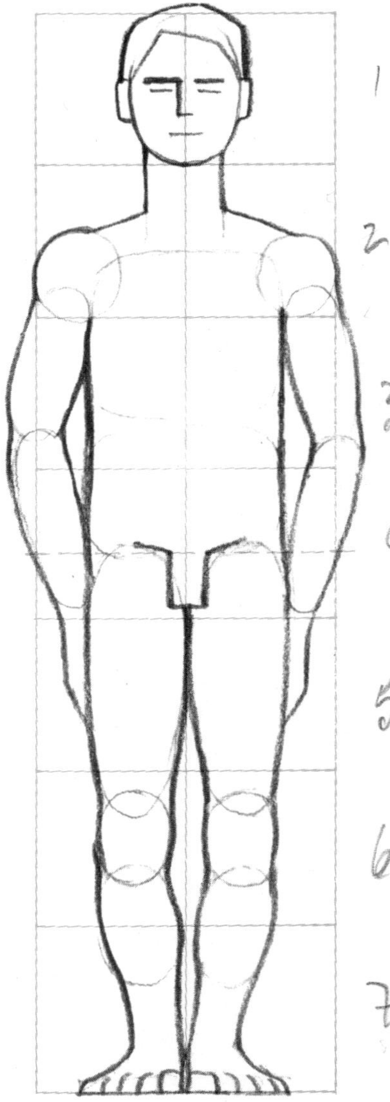

Different builds

By changing the number of 'head-lengths' the build of the body can be altered. If nine 'head-lengths' are used the dimensions are increased. This is how a very tall person would appear. The middle of the body is then four-and-a-half 'head-lengths' down.

However, for a small, fat person only seven 'head-lengths' are necessary.

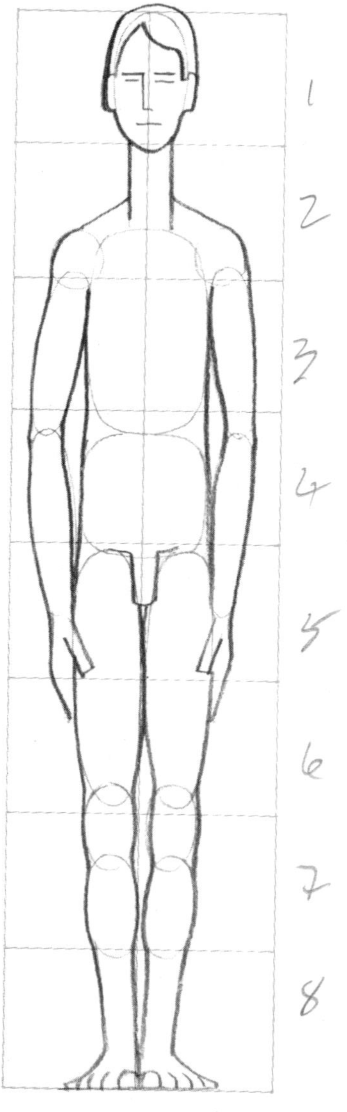

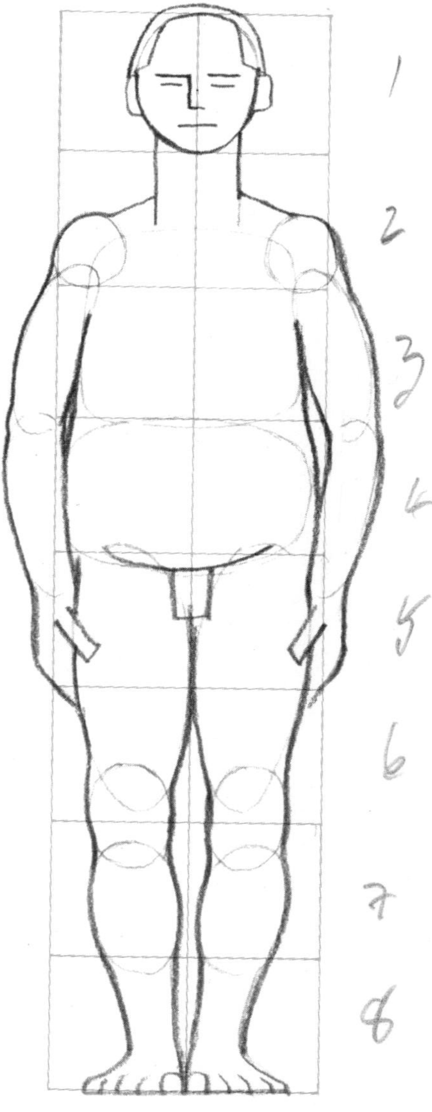

But it is possible to draw the various body builds by using the eight-part basic model. This can be done by changing the proportions. For instance, with a slim person the chest and abdomen are narrow. This means turning the squares of the graph into rectangles.

For a fat person the squares are 'squashed' a little.

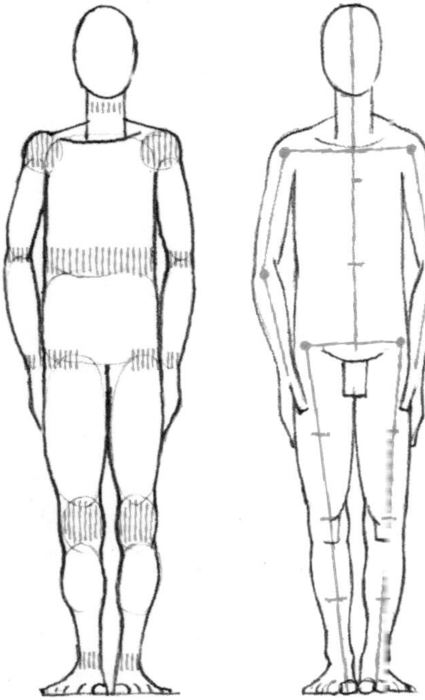

Now the figure can be set in motion. But, because a person can move many different parts of his body — for example, the shoulder joints, knees, hips, backbone — a simple mechanism is necessary: the body's axis. By using it, the positions of the various parts of the body can be drawn more precisely. The 'head-lengths' are marked on the axis. In this way the correct proportions can be achieved, even when the body is in motion.

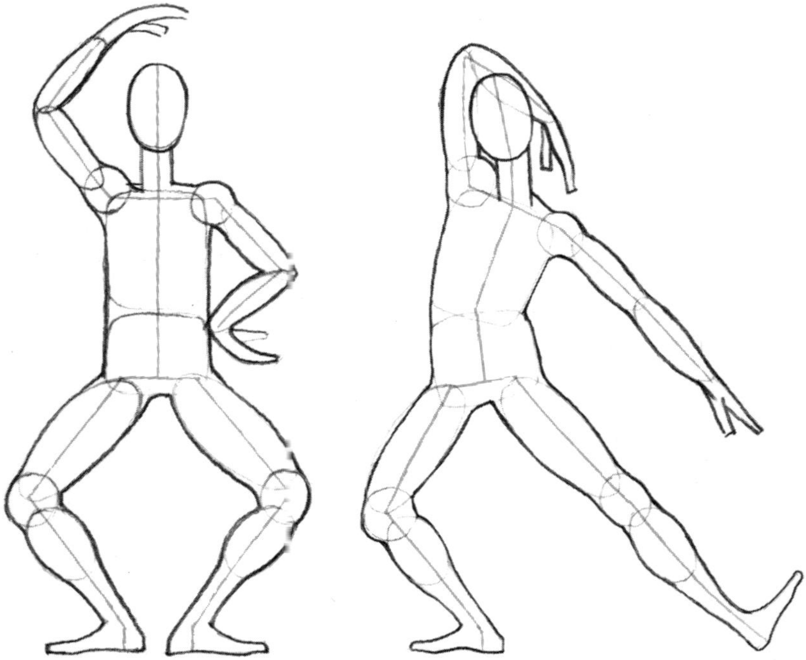

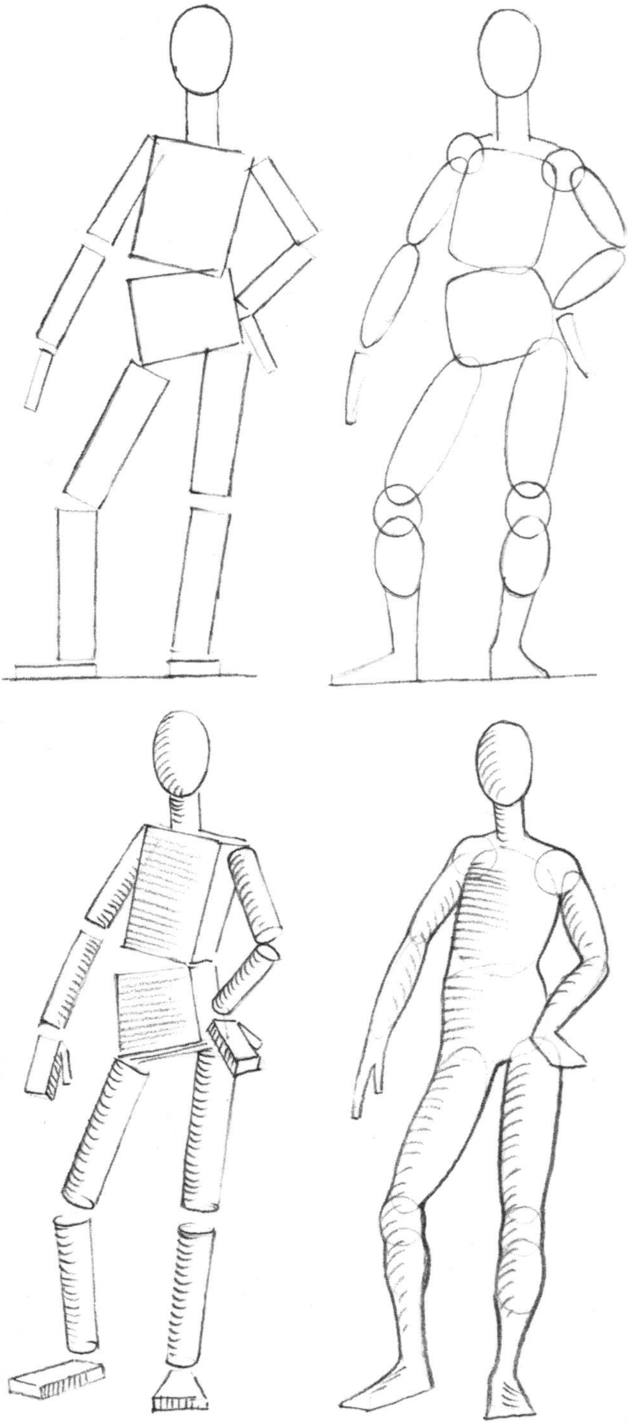

Place all the body weight on one leg, thus shifting the axis. The heel of the weight-bearing leg lies on a vertical line starting at the nape of the neck.

Notice that on this side the body has a sharp bend. The axes of the shoulders and the abdomen come closer together.

Now try three-dimensional drawings of these movements.

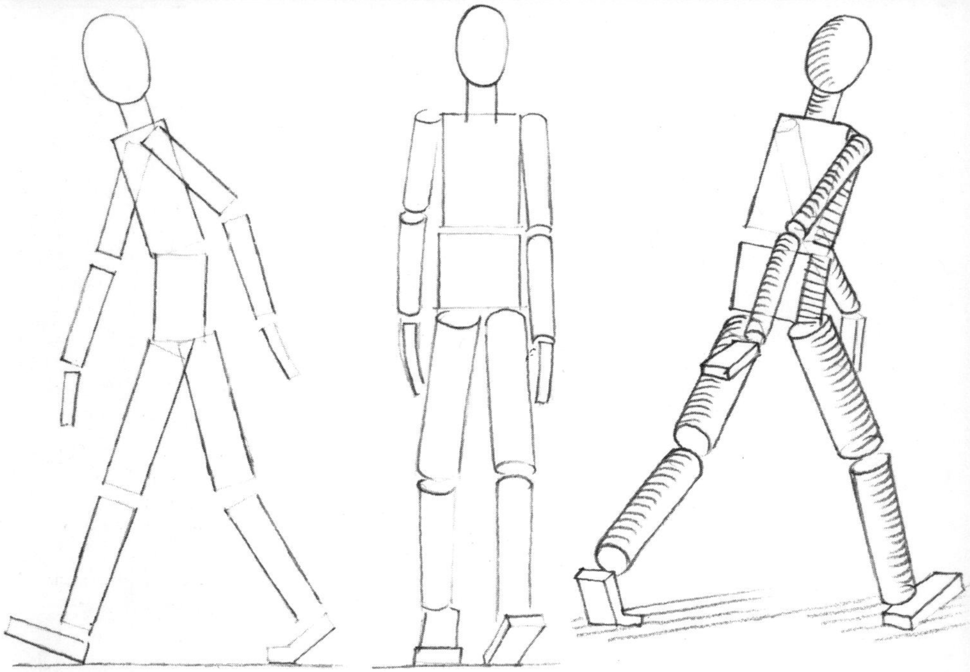

Draw a man walking. His movements are balanced: when he puts his right foot forward, he swings his right arm back.

Draw the man from the side, from the front, and then in three dimensions.

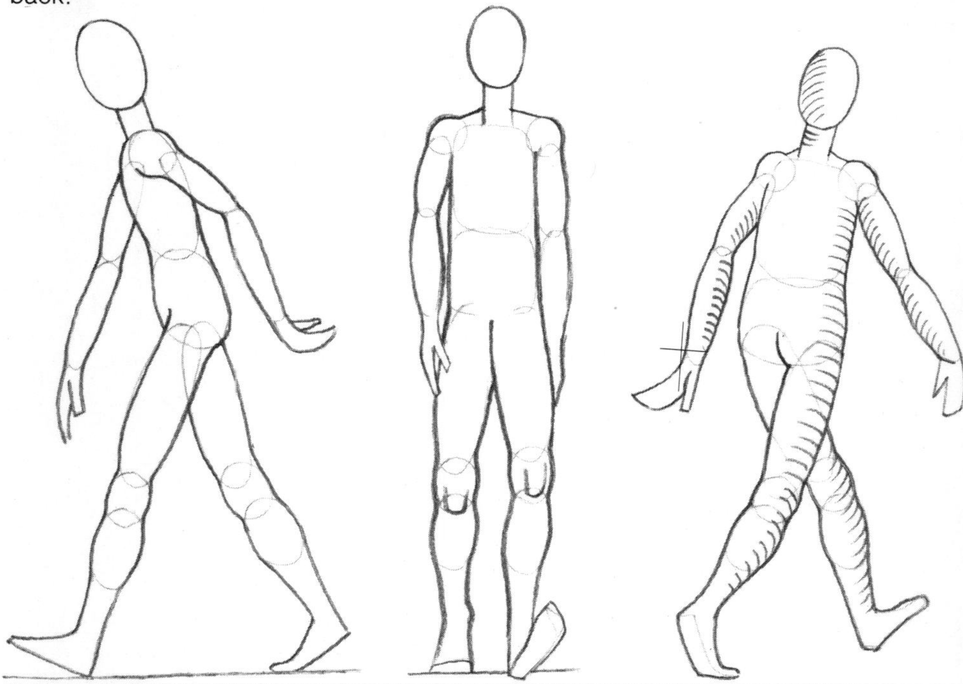

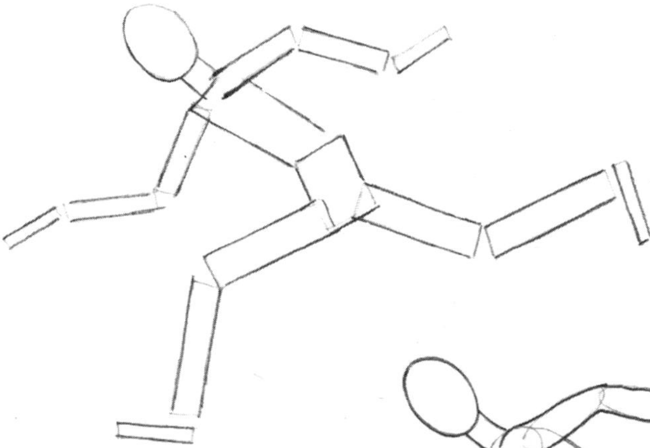

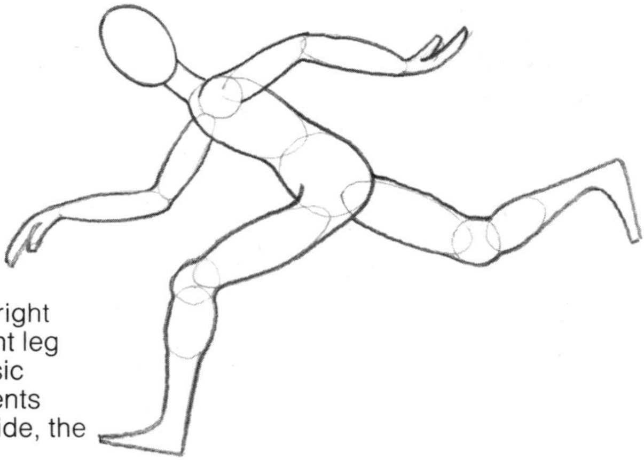

It is the same with running: the right arm goes forward when the right leg goes back. Again, use your basic model and draw these movements from various angles: from the side, the front, and in three dimensions.

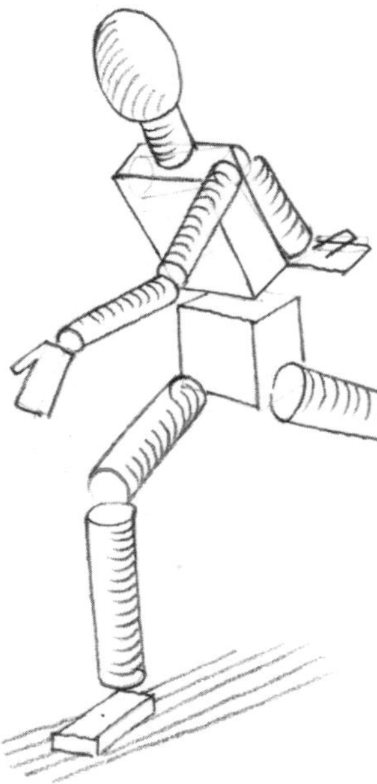

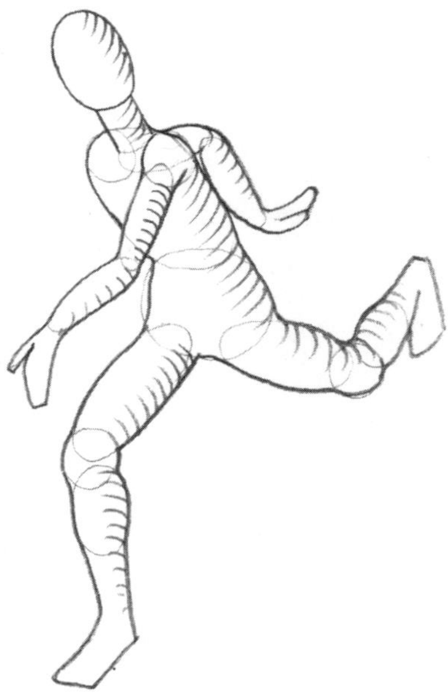

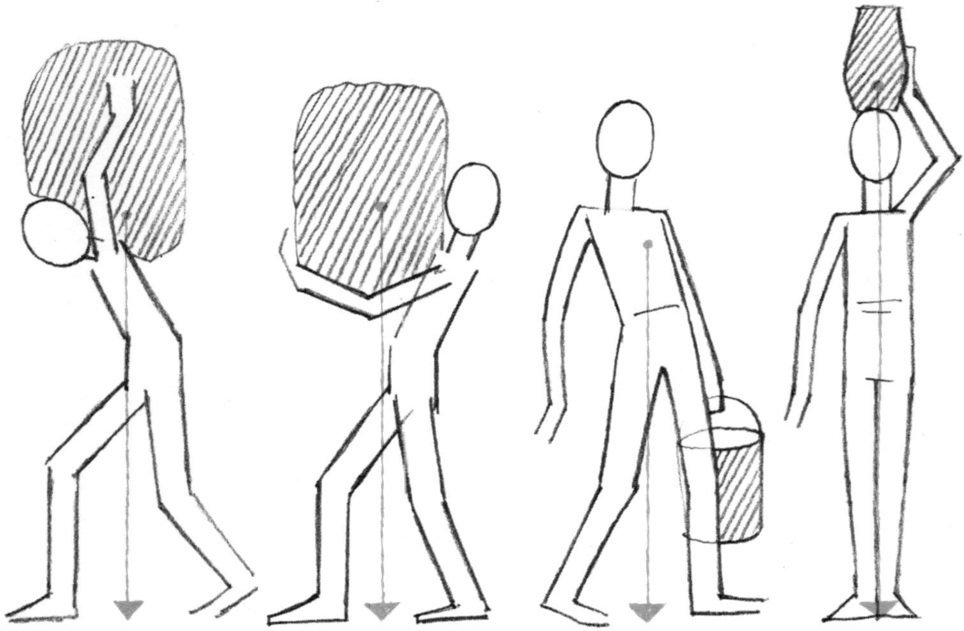

When carrying things, a person constantly adjusts his movements to maintain balance. His centre of gravity changes all the time.

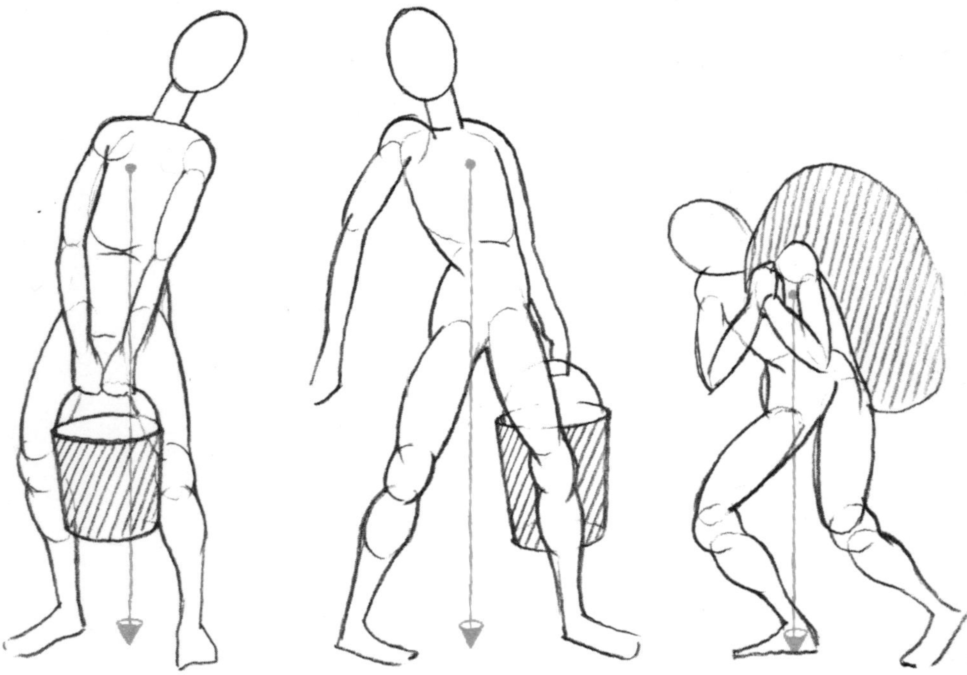

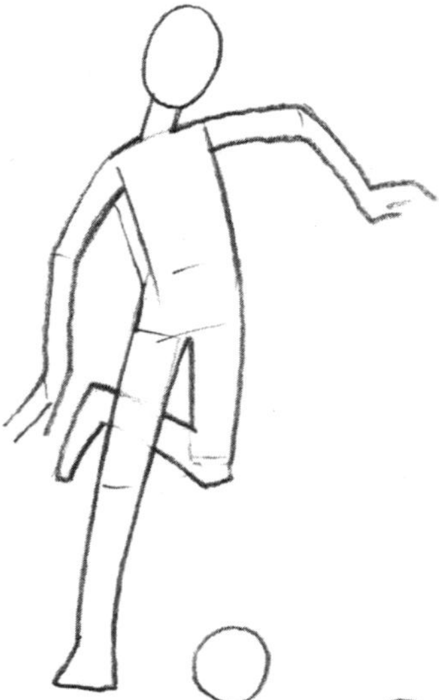

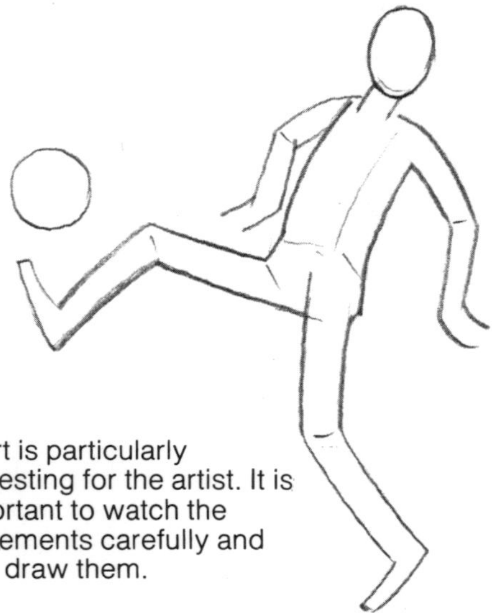

Sport is particularly interesting for the artist. It is important to watch the movements carefully and then draw them.

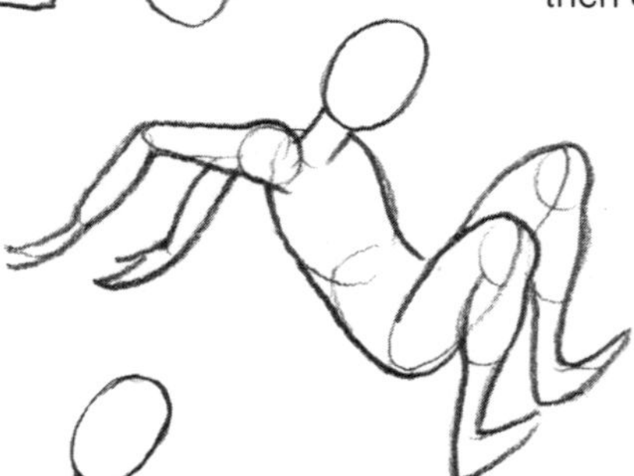

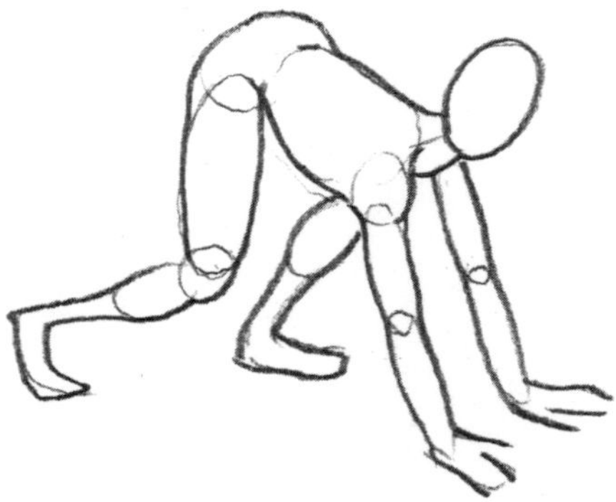

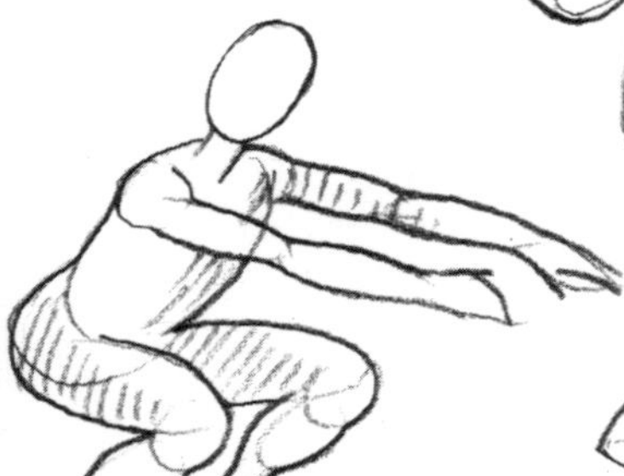

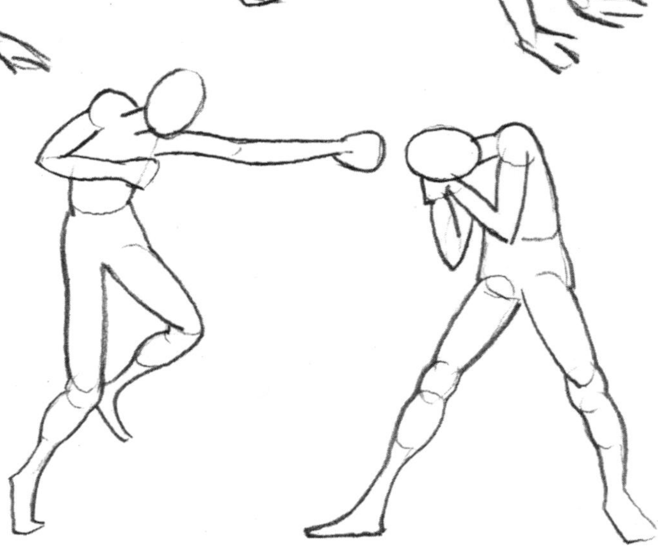

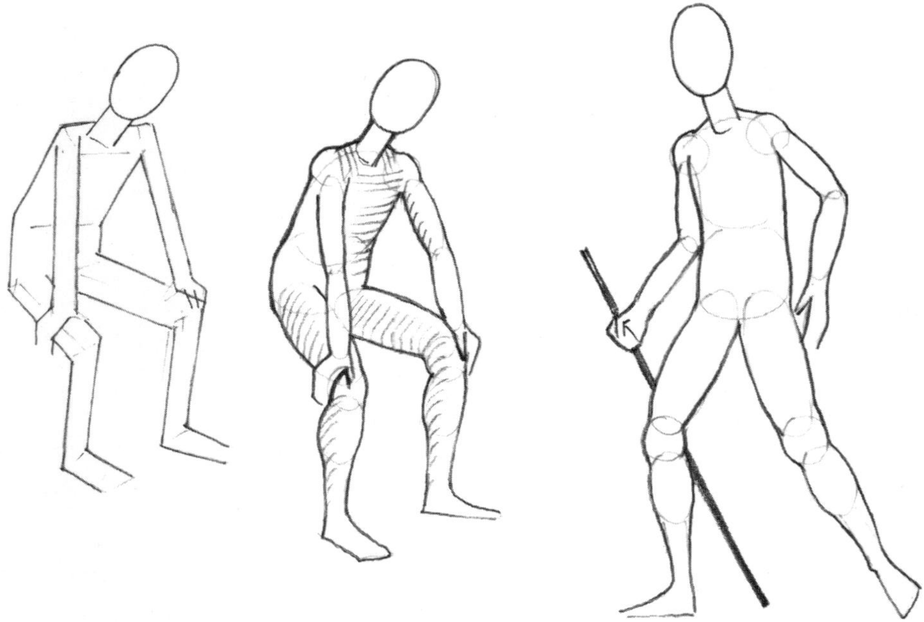

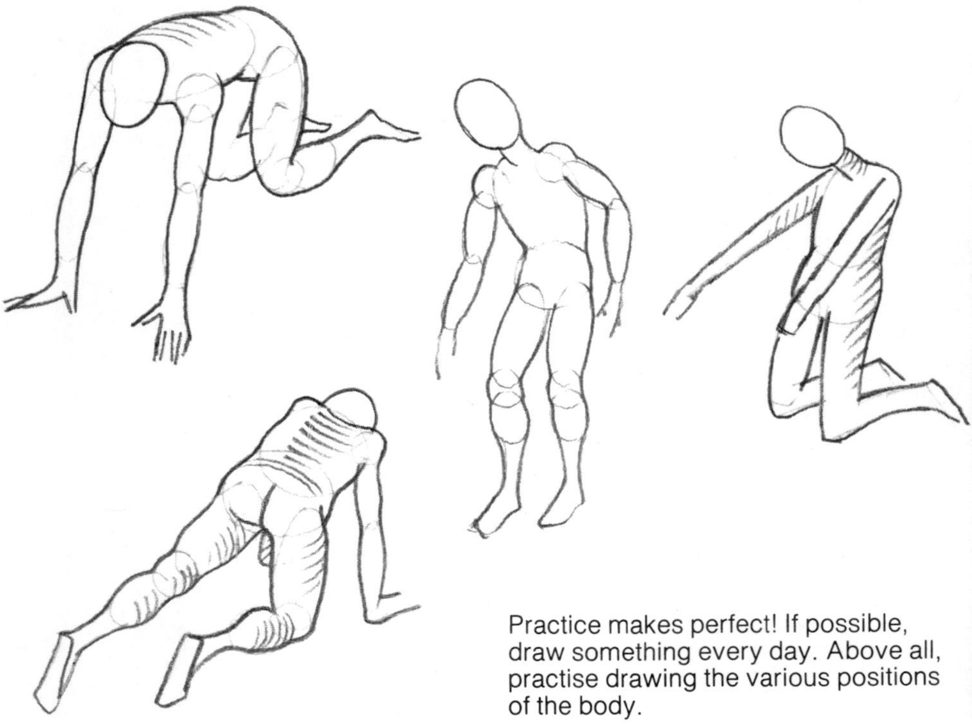

Practice makes perfect! If possible, draw something every day. Above all, practise drawing the various positions of the body.

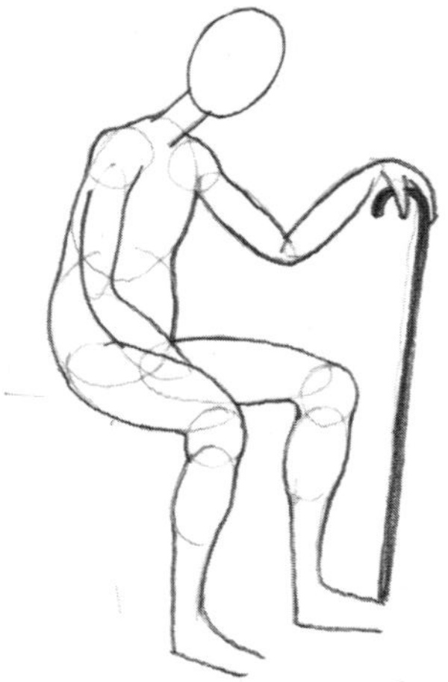

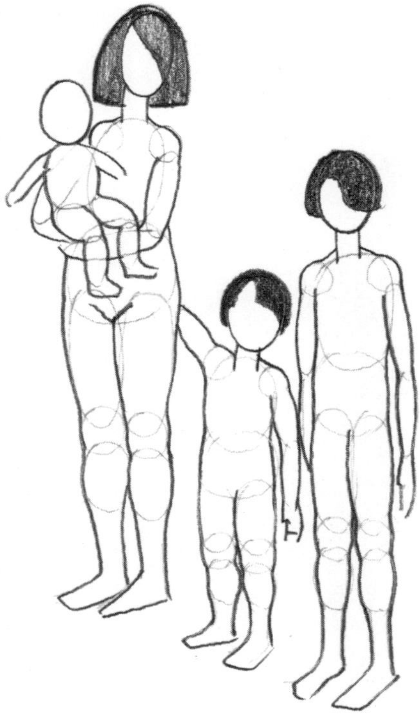

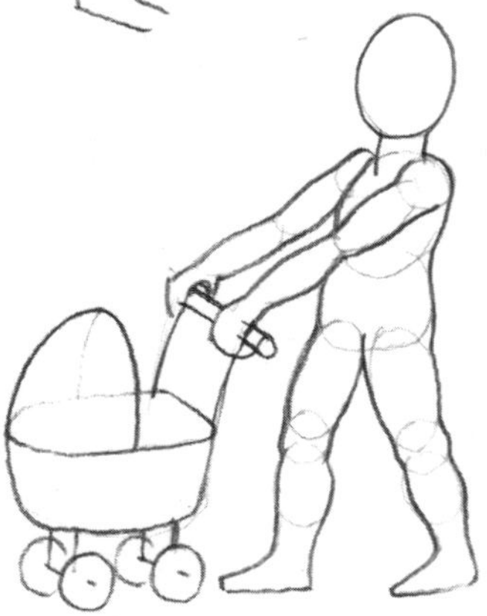

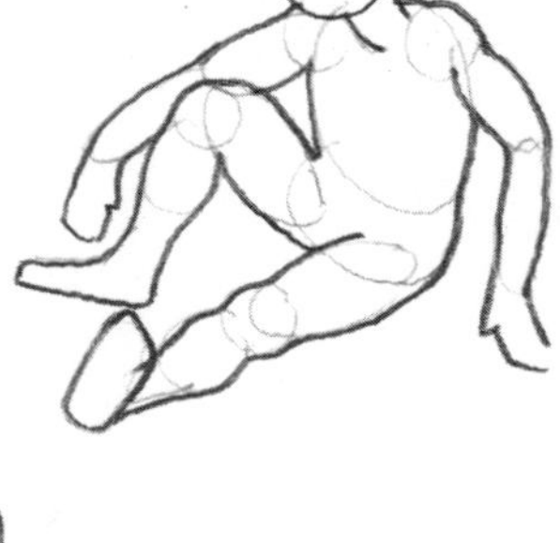

Now use everything you have learnt so far.

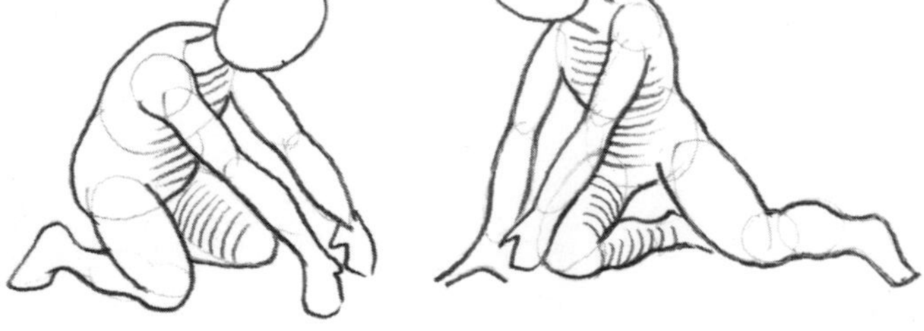

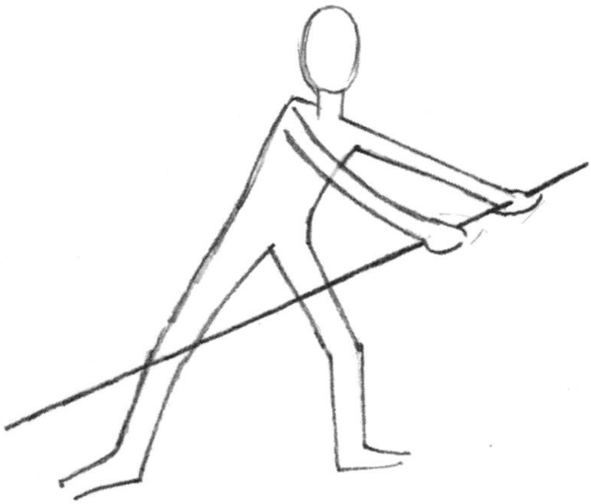

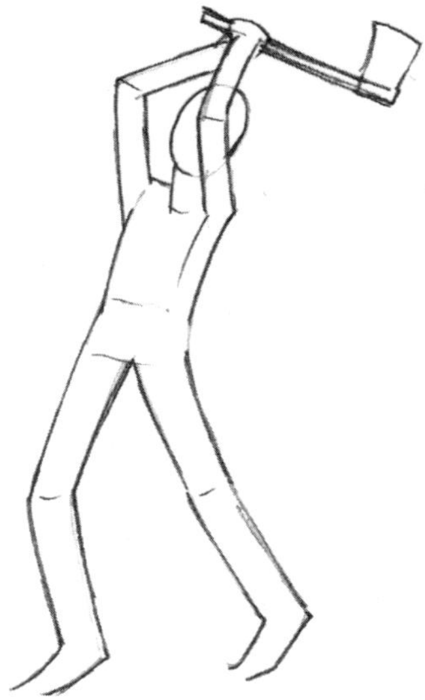

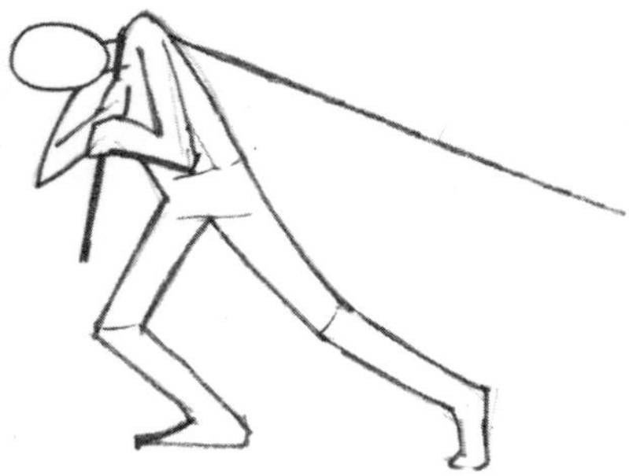

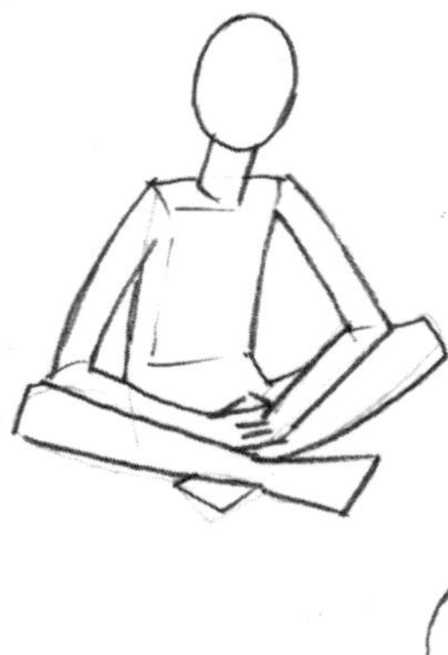

Draw figures performing various actions: use the basic geometric shapes.

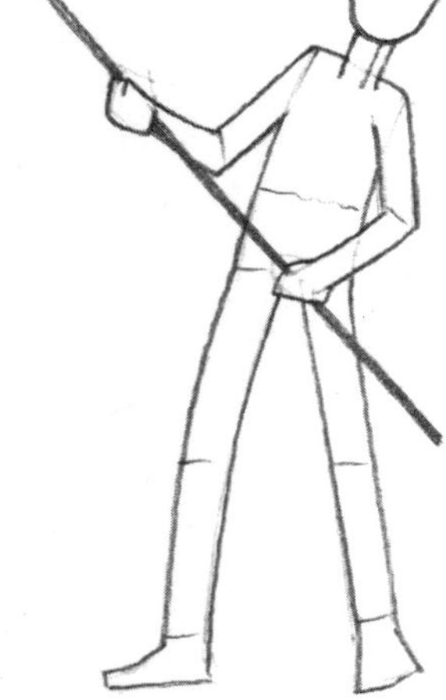

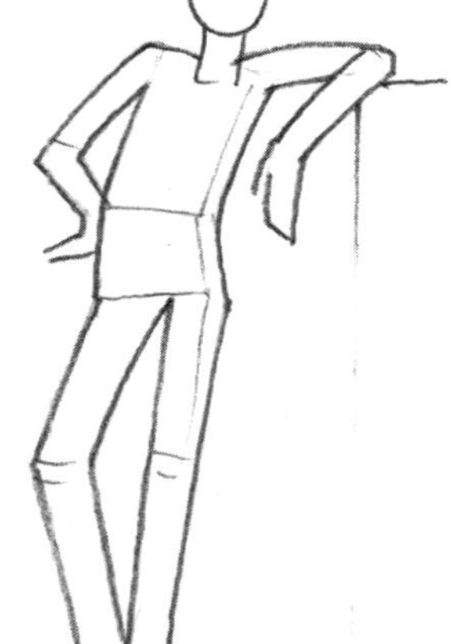

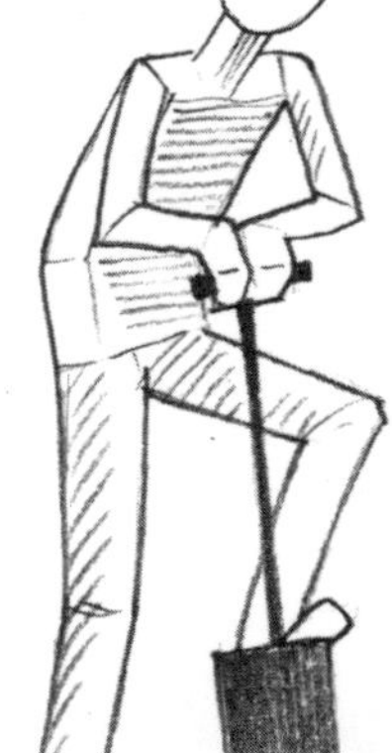

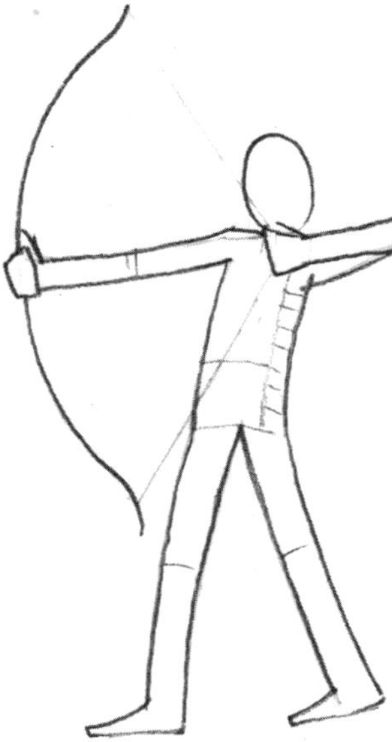

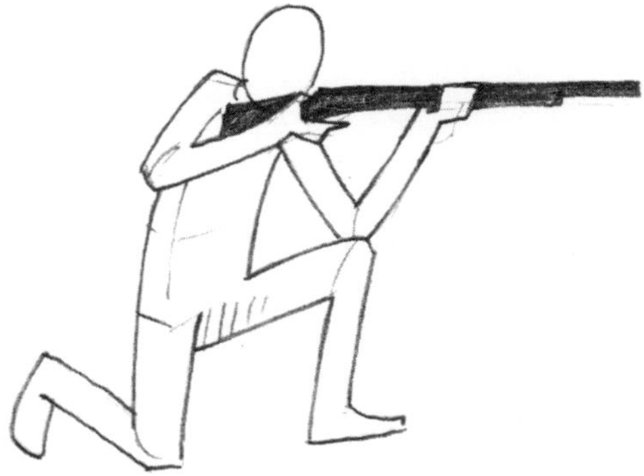

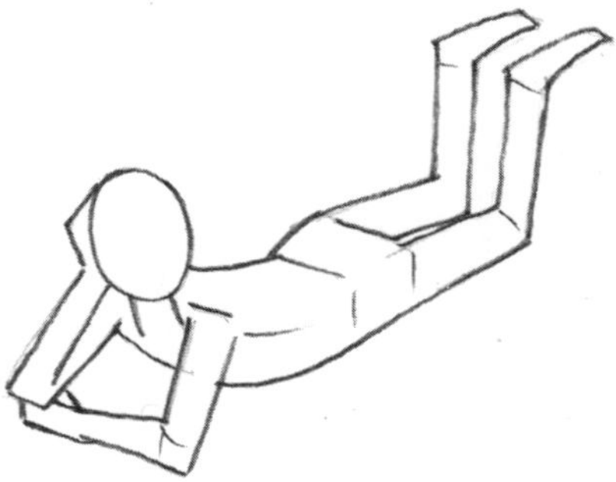

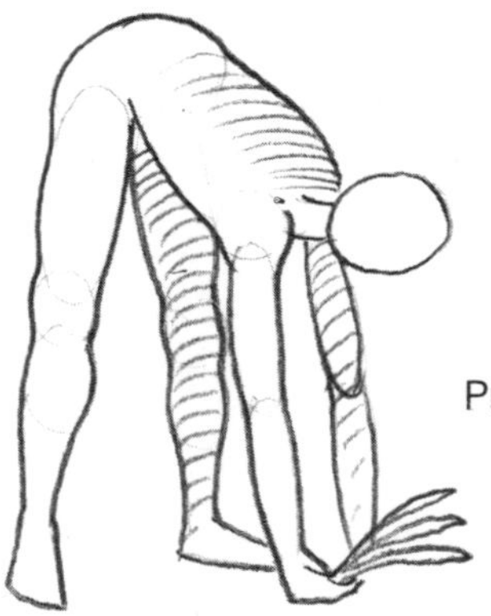

Practise using shading.

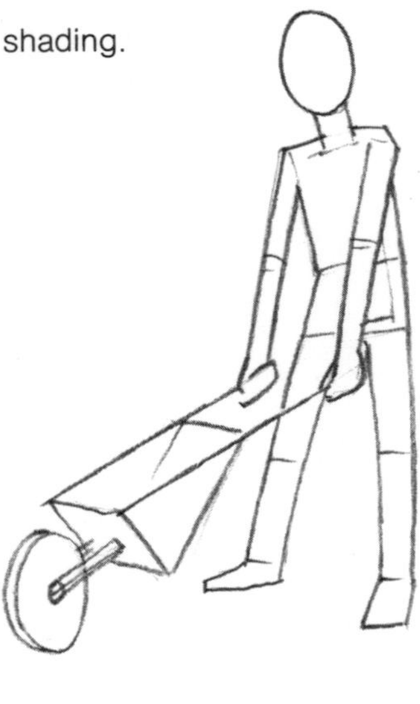

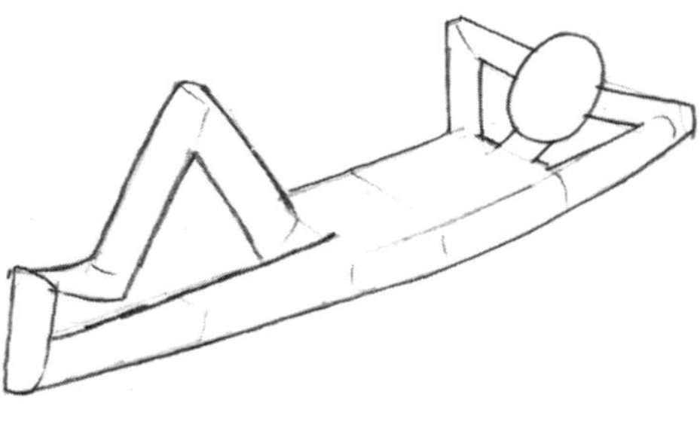

Now for the details:

The head

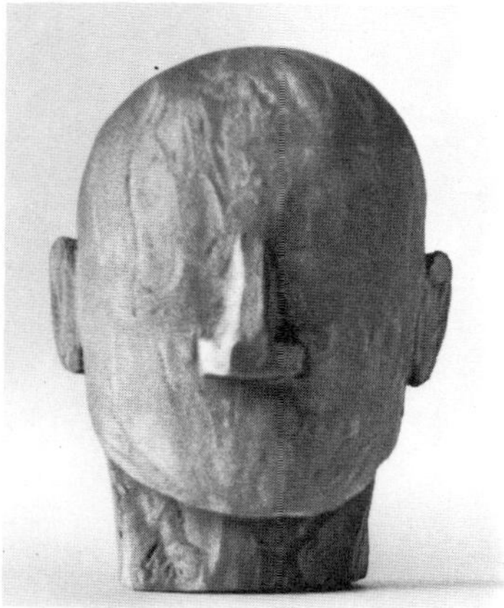

As you can see, the head is basically a sphere with a shield-like face.

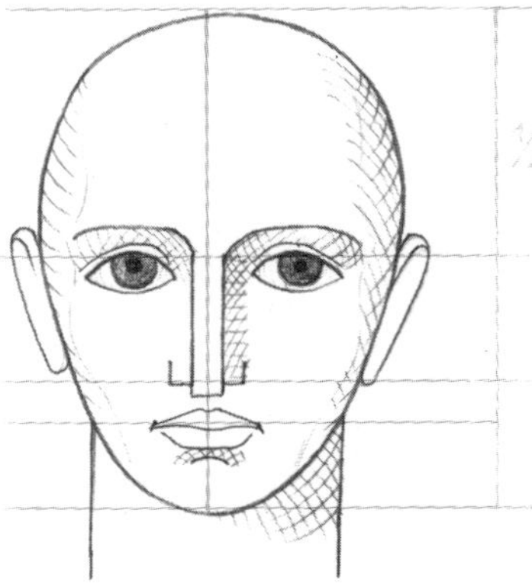

The head can be viewed as an ellipse, and divided by a vertical line down the middle. Horizontal lines can be added for the eyes, nose and mouth.

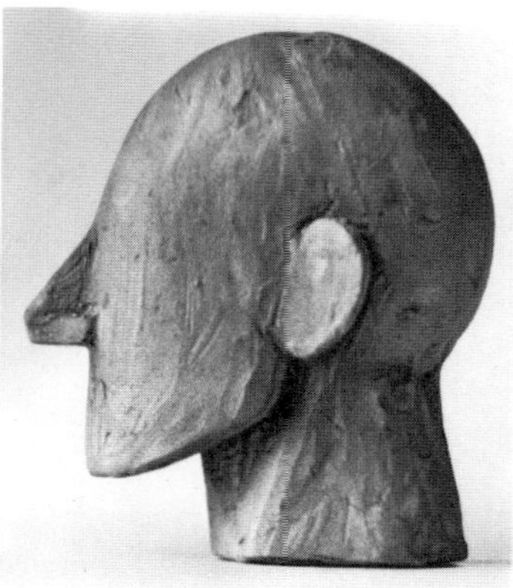

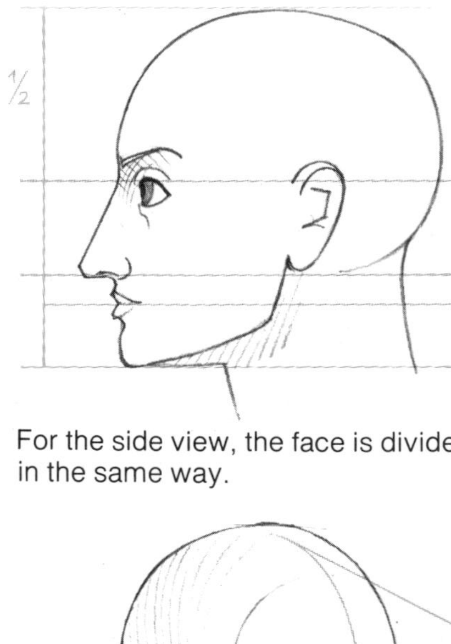

For the side view, the face is divided in the same way.

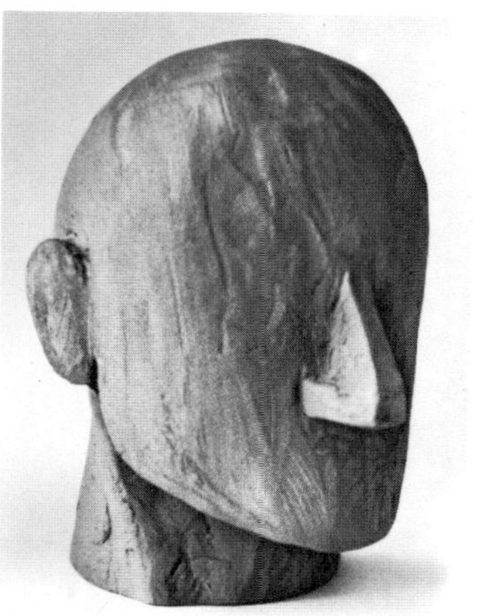

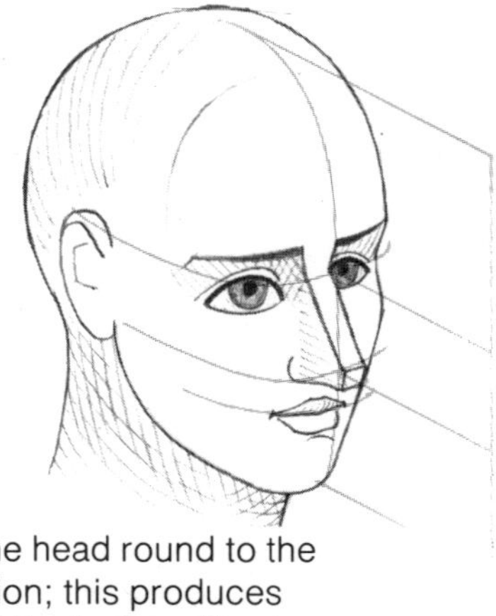

Slowly turn the head round to the original position; this produces what is called the half-profile view.

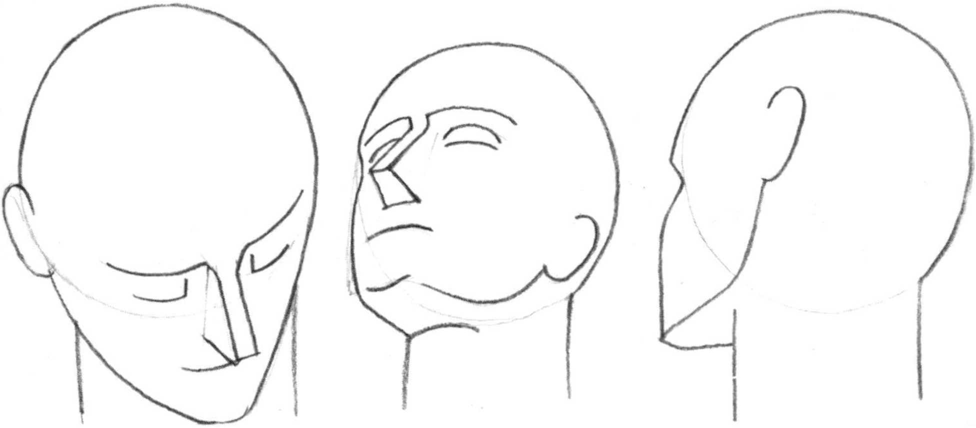

Practise drawing the head in different positions.

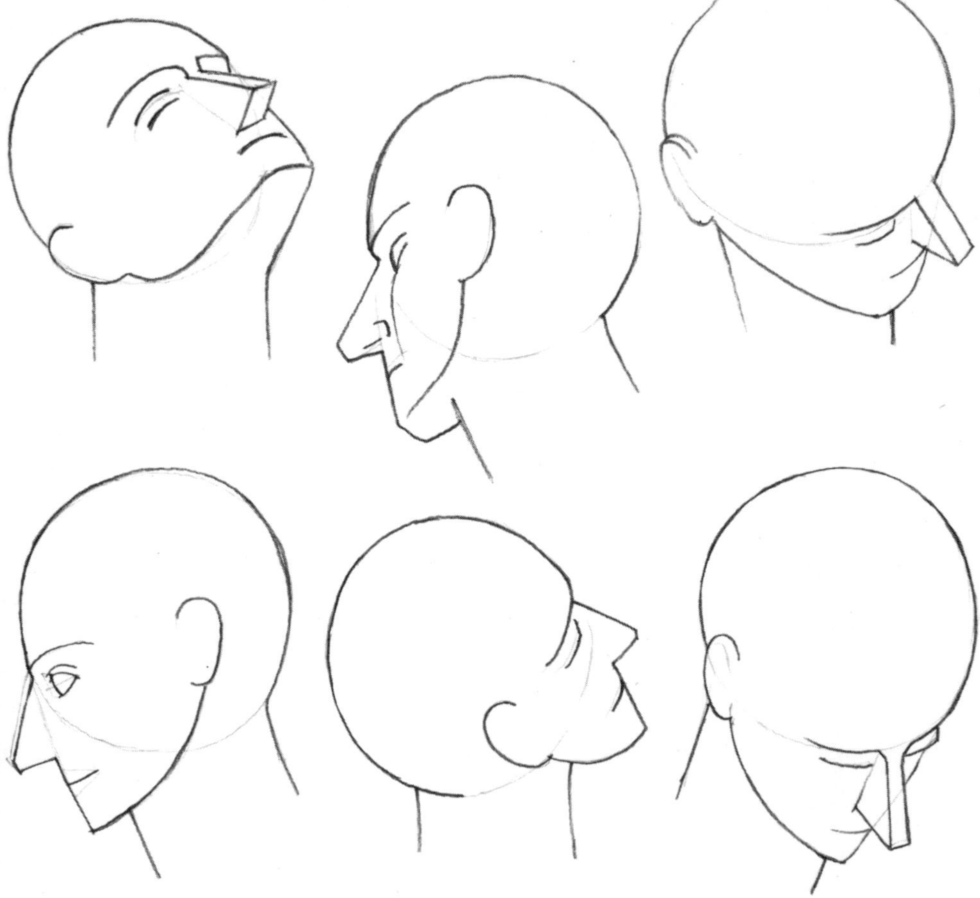

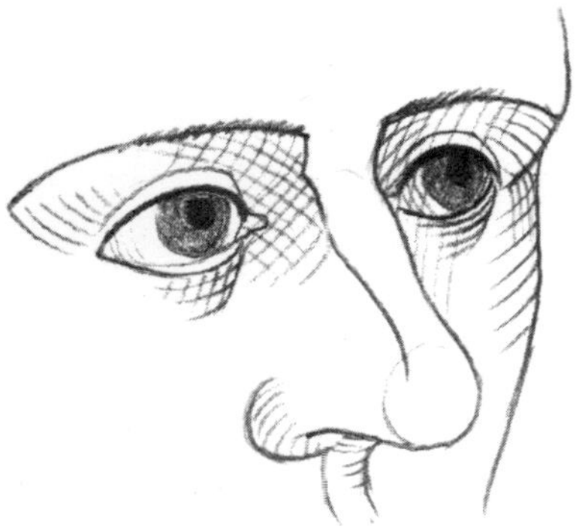

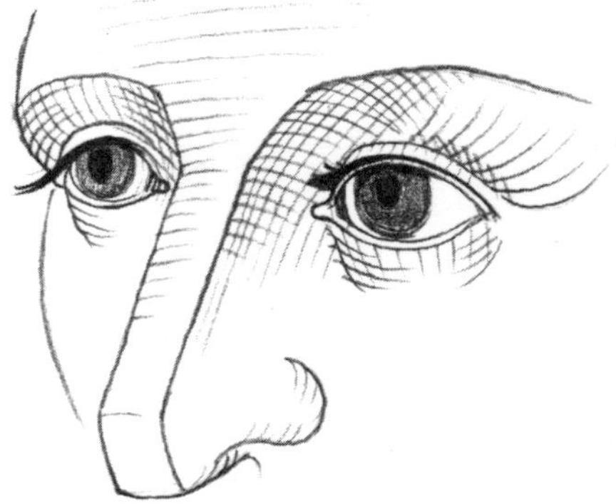

The eye

The eye is shaped like a ball and is framed by the upper and lower eyelids. When it is open, there is a horizontal fold over it. The line of vision of both eyes is always parallel.

The nose

Seen simply, the nose forms a triangle. But, if it is drawn in three dimensions, lines parallel to the ridge of the nose are necessary. Then the nostrils are added at the side. Practise different types of noses.

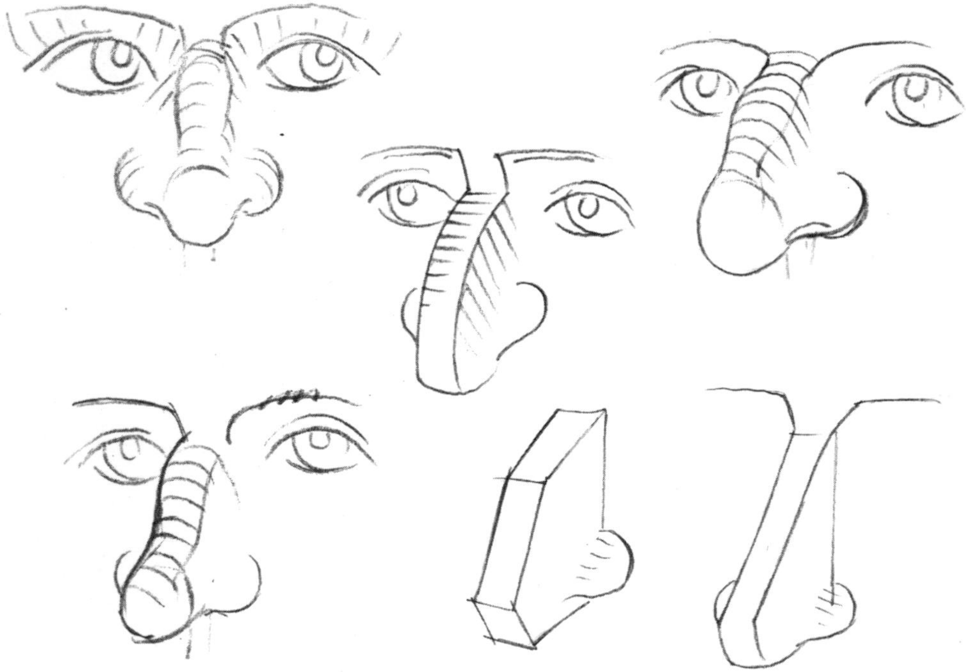

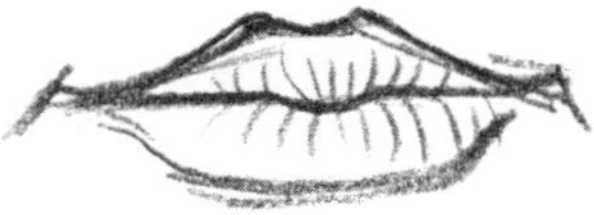

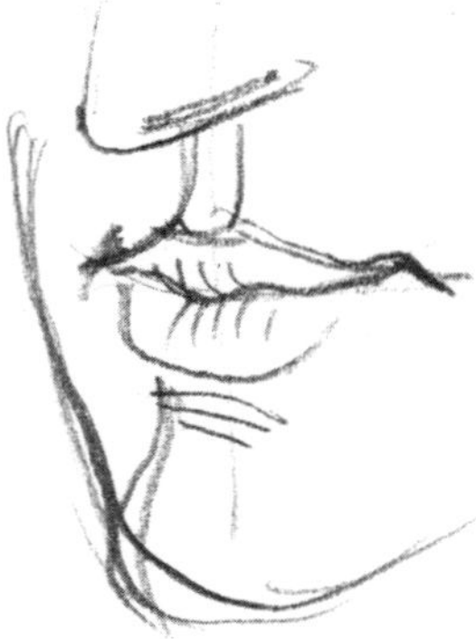

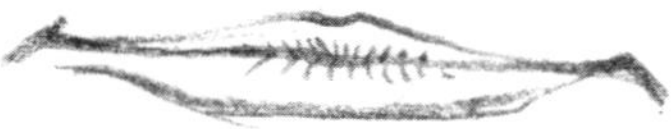

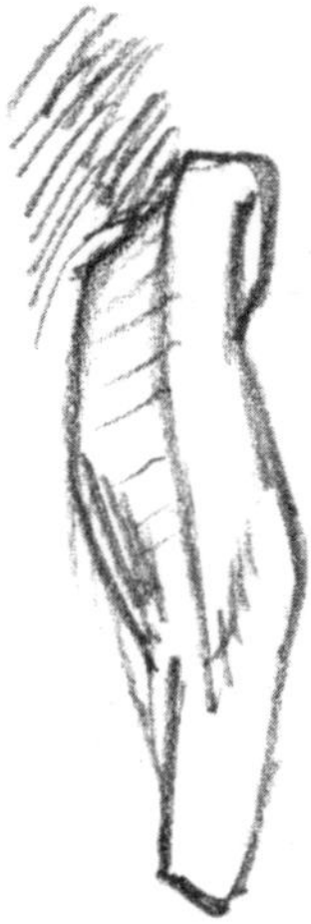

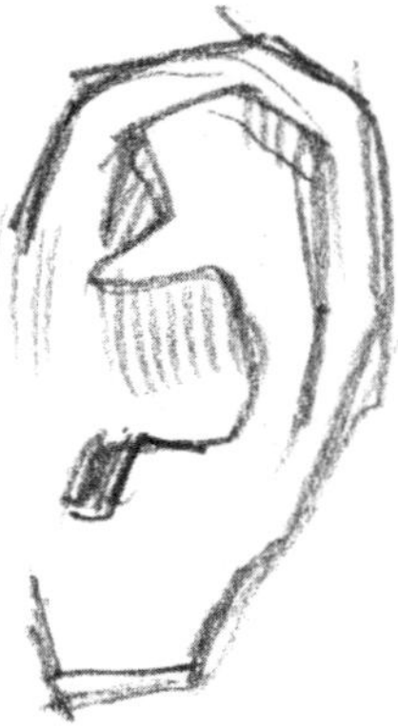

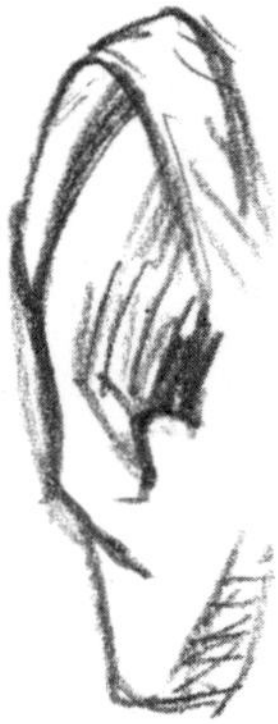

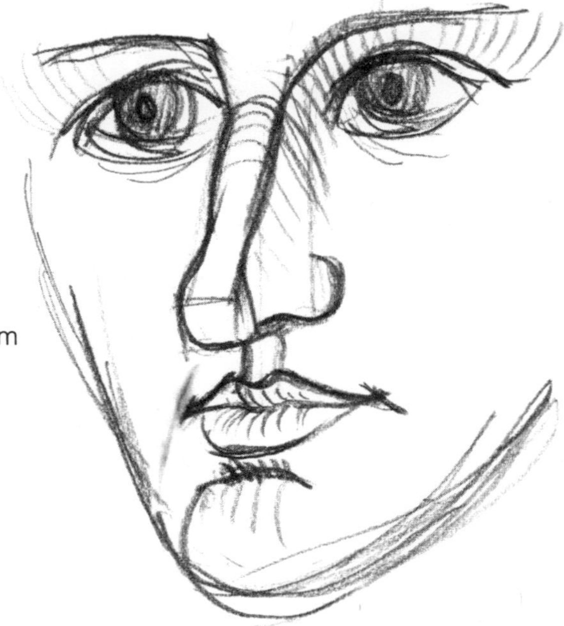

The mouth

Firstly, practise drawing the lips from the front until you can get them as close to perfect as possible. Then draw them from different angles.

The ear

The ear is particularly hard to draw. For this reason, try to find the basic geometric shape.

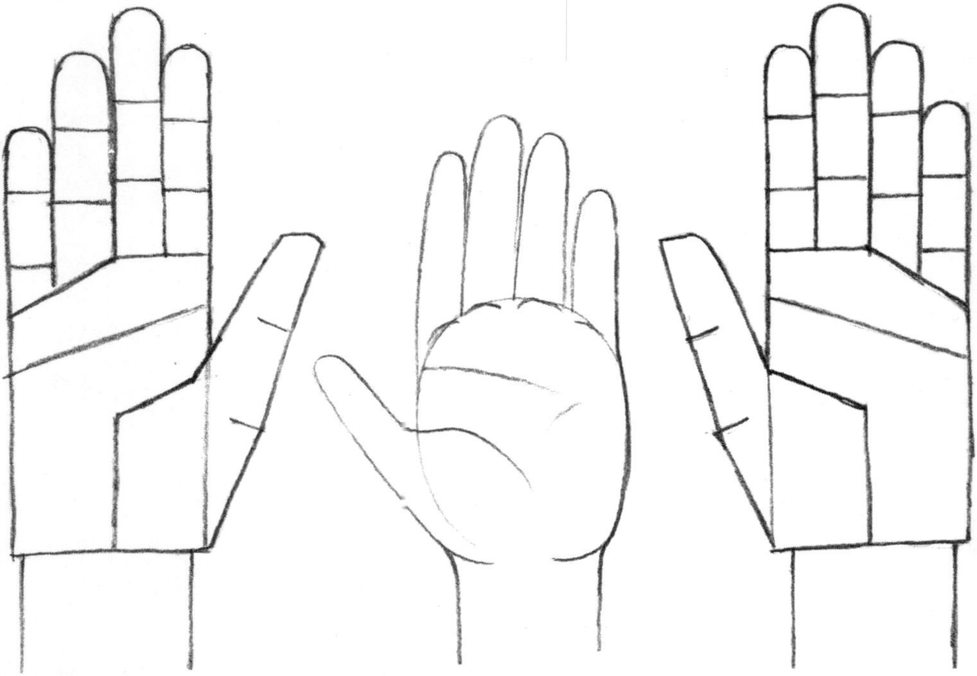

The hand

The fingers are of different lengths, the longest one being the middle finger. The thumb is attached further down the 'slab' and can move in directions different from the other fingers.

The hand converts easily into a geometric shape: a slab-like formation which may be rounded or angular.

Perspective can also be used to draw this slab.

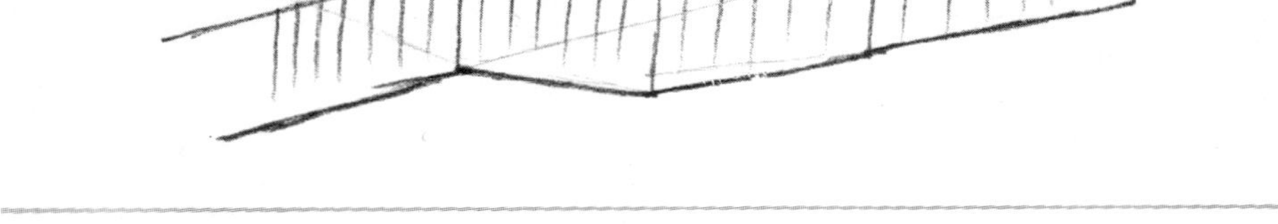

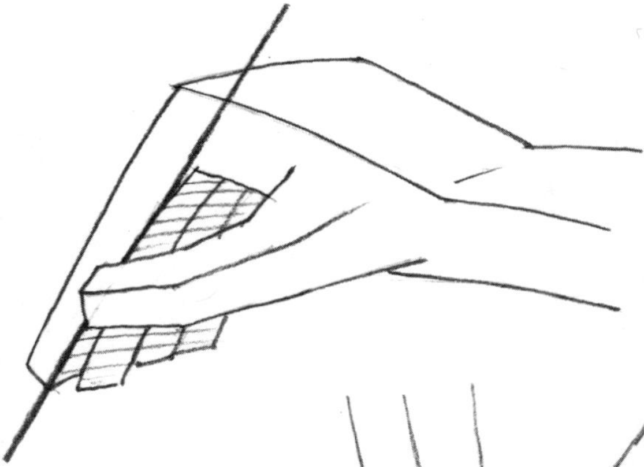

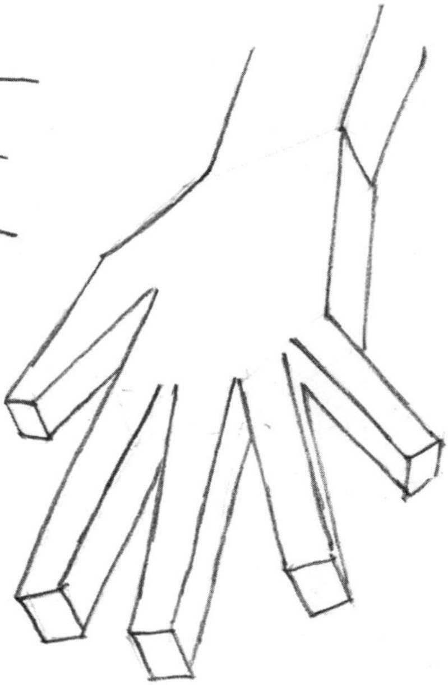

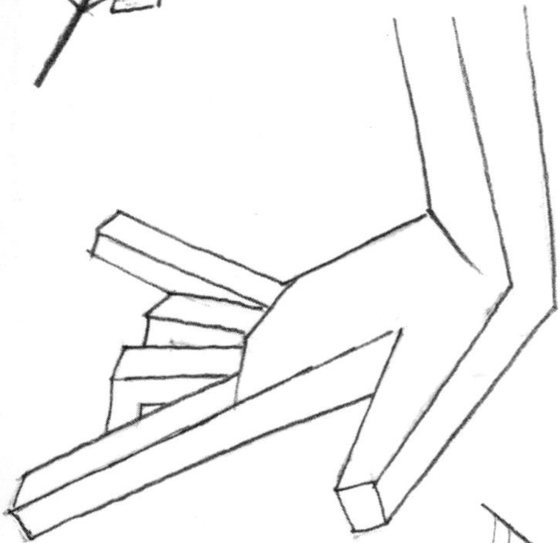

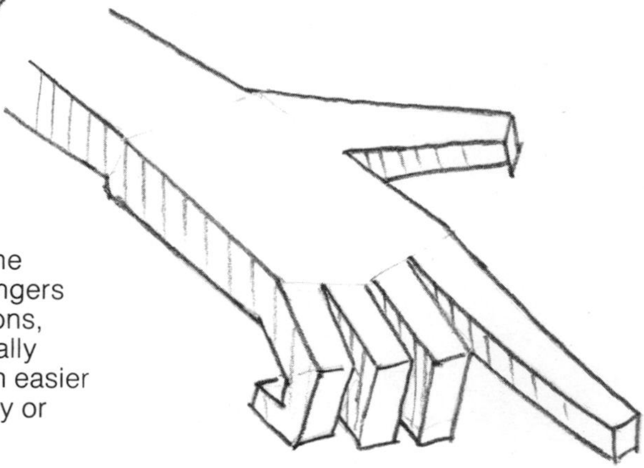

In the next step, try to bring some movement into the hand. The fingers can be splayed out in all directions, and each finger can be individually bent in different ways. It is much easier if you first model the hand in clay or plasticine.

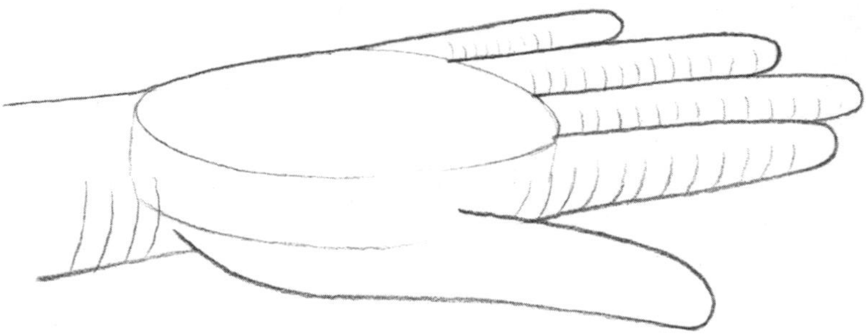

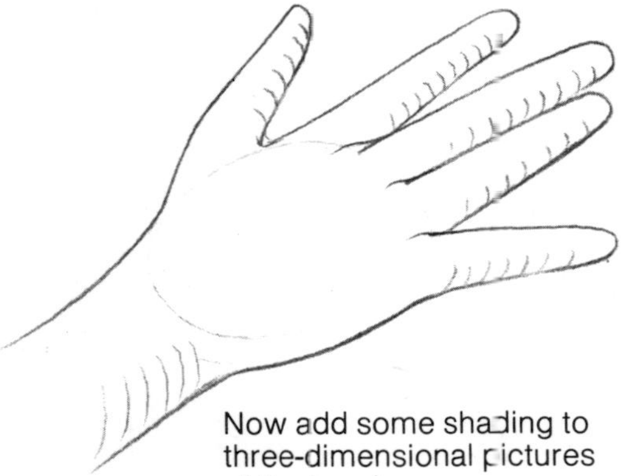

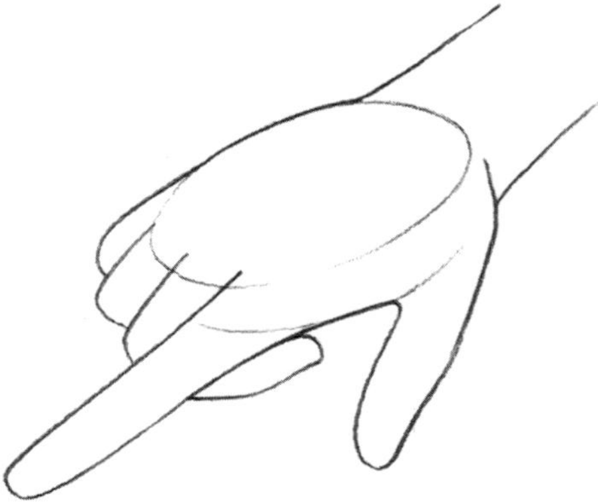

Now add some shading to three-dimensional pictures of the hand.

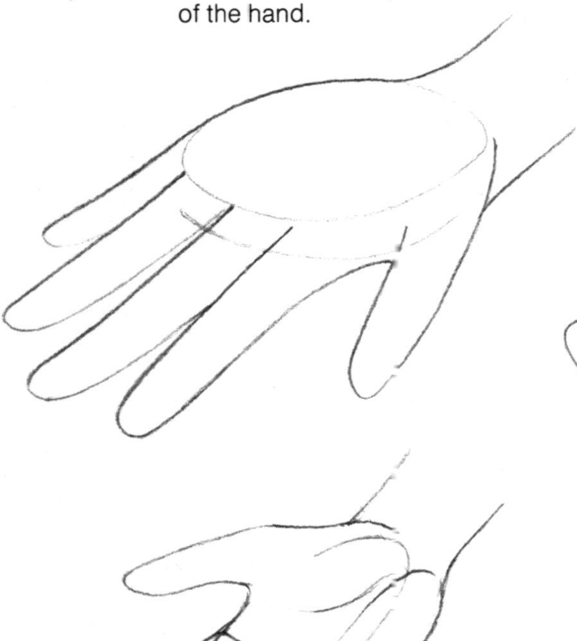

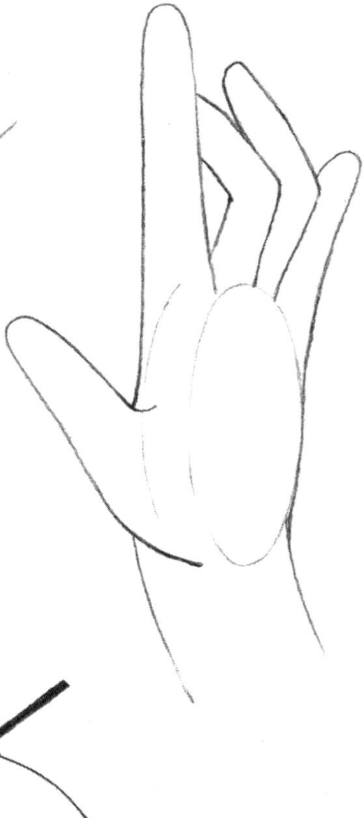

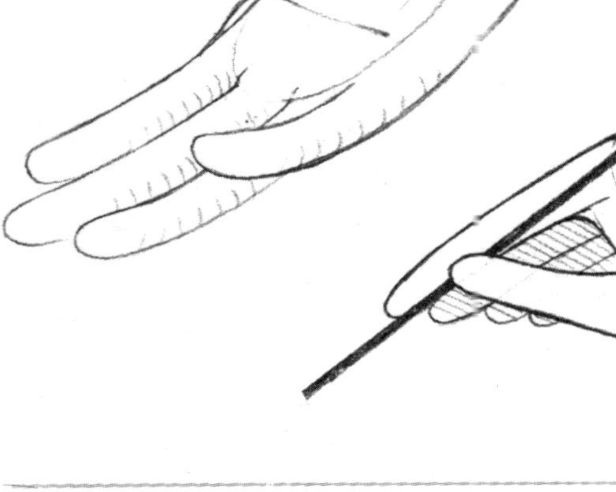

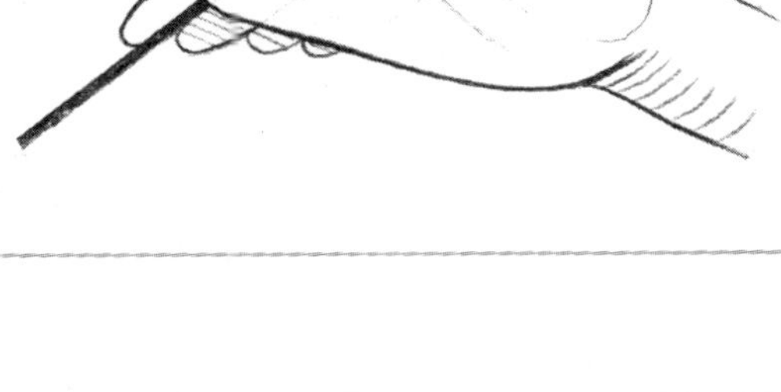

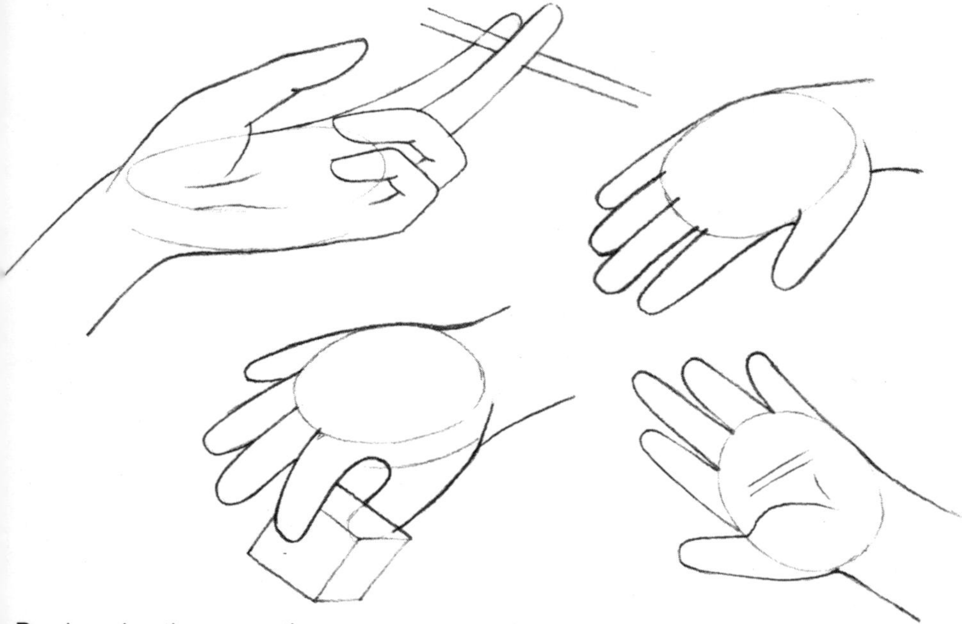

By changing the proportions, you can create different types of hands. A woman's hand may have longer, more slender fingers. A child's hand has shorter, rounder fingers. Wide, angular fingers usually belong to someone who works with his hands.

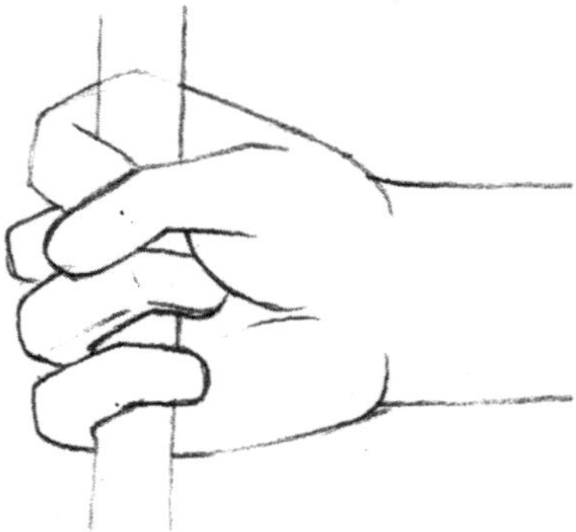

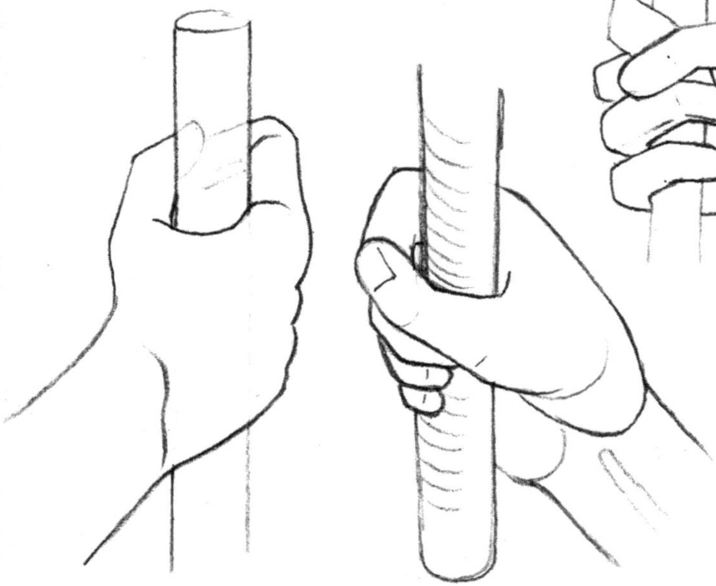

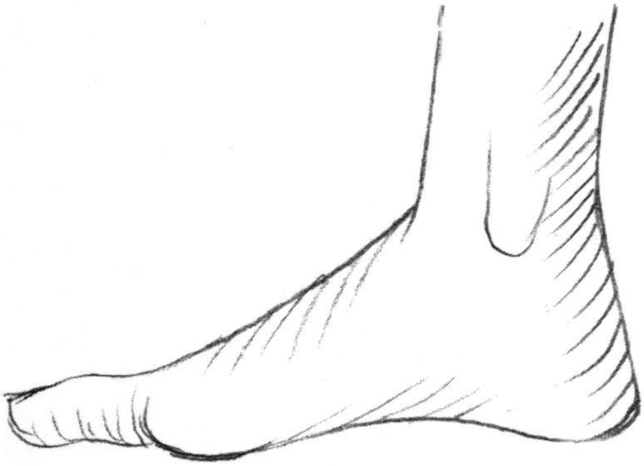

The foot

Just as for the hand, start with a simplified geometric shape.

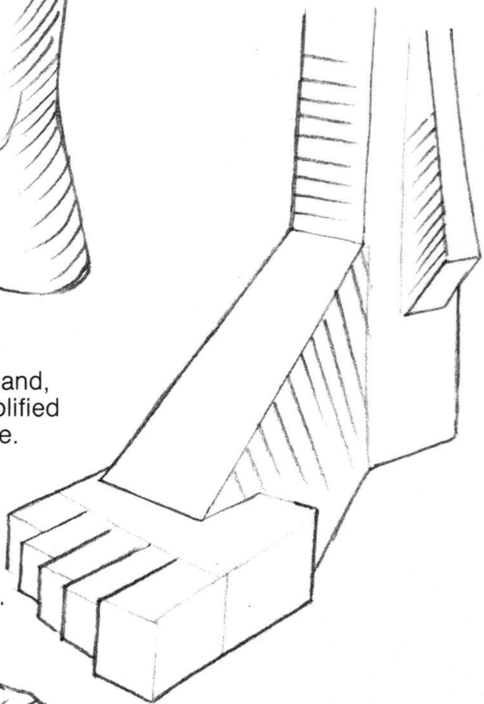

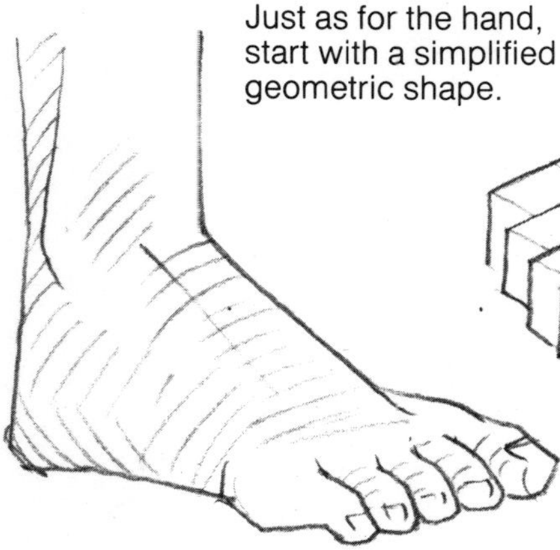

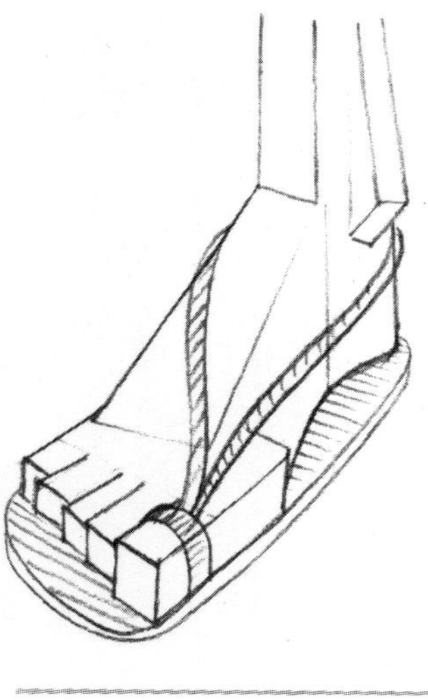

Now put the foot into a shoe, remembering that the position of the foot will vary according to whether the shoe is flat or not.

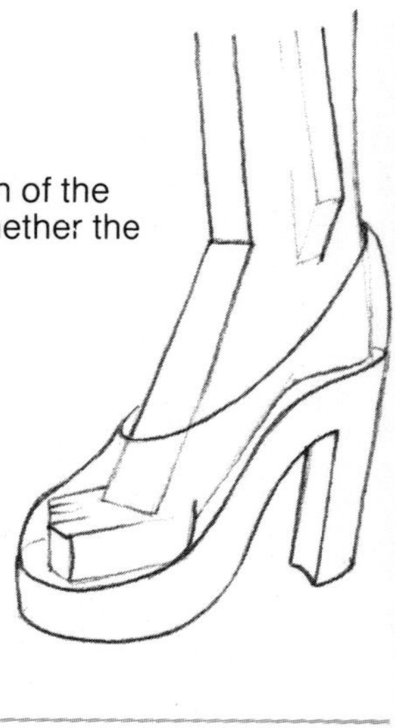

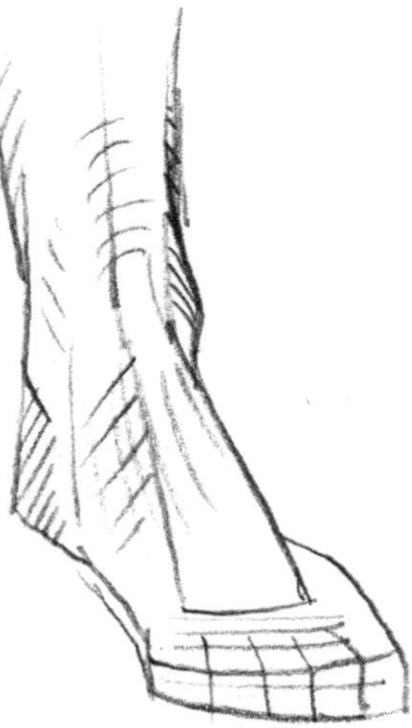

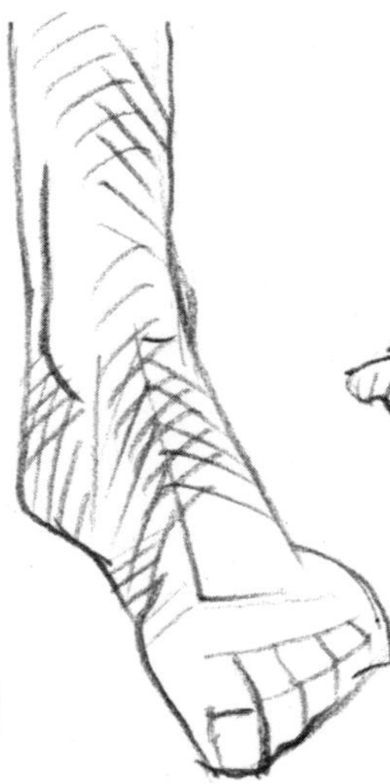

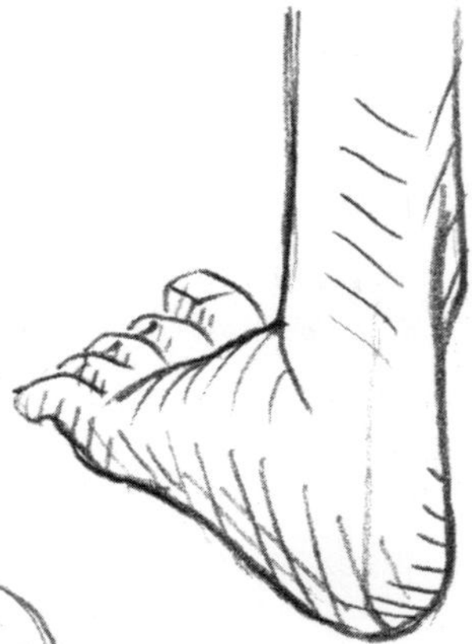

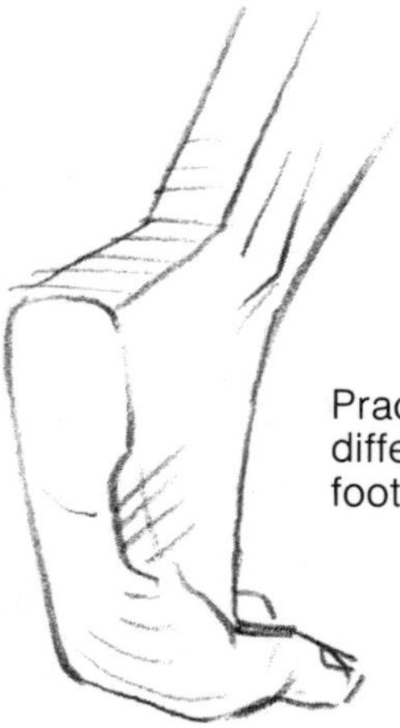

Practise drawing the foot from different angles. Then draw the foot walking.

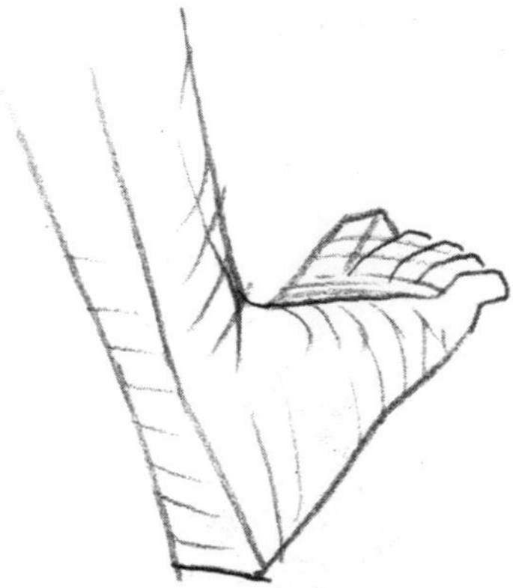

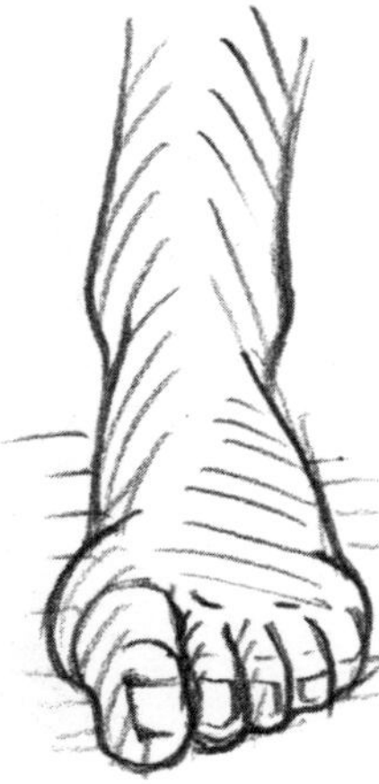

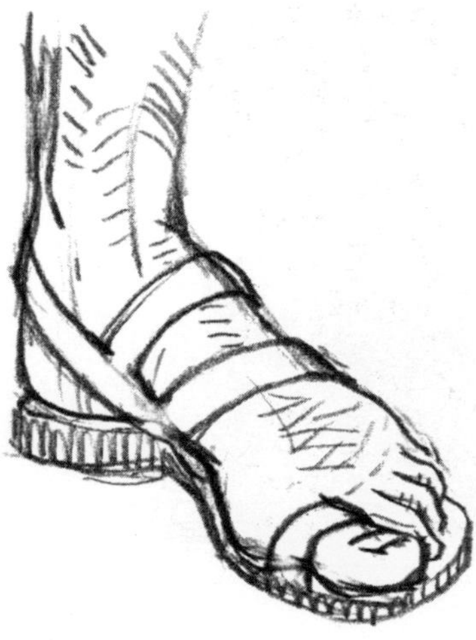

Now put into practice everything you have learnt; try to draw freely.

Combine all the elements of expression and movement, including clothing.

You can adapt or change your basic model — don't allow yourself to become too bound by it.

The mark of a good drawing is how life-like it appears. First of all, do a sketch with a soft pencil. The lines should freely and effortlessly follow the structure you have already learnt (see the examples).

These sketches form the basis for further drawings. Place a piece of transparent paper on top of the sketches so that you can add any necessary corrections or variations. In this way, a carefully drawn picture emerges.

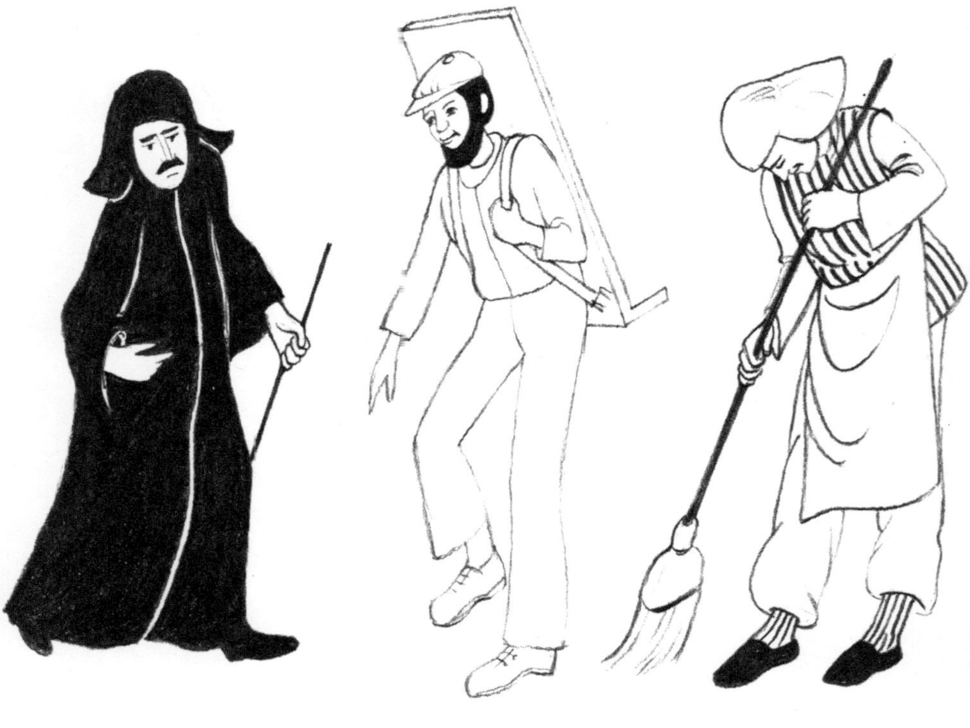

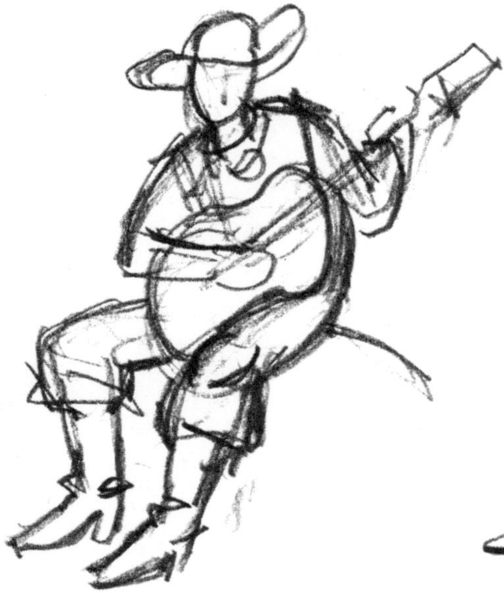

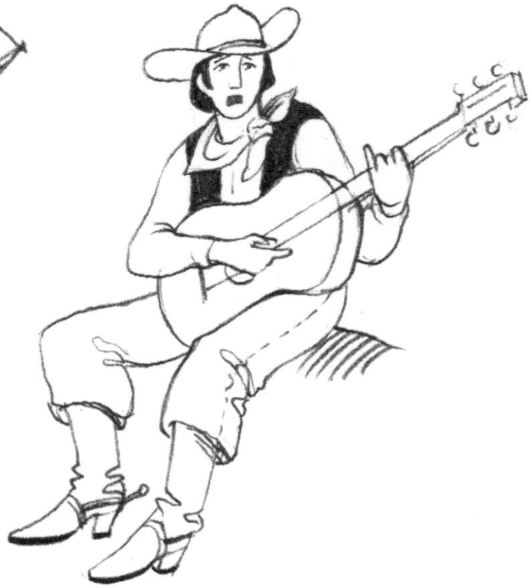

The addition of clothing provides a more interesting, varied picture: such details give people their individual characteristics.

There are more examples on the following pages.

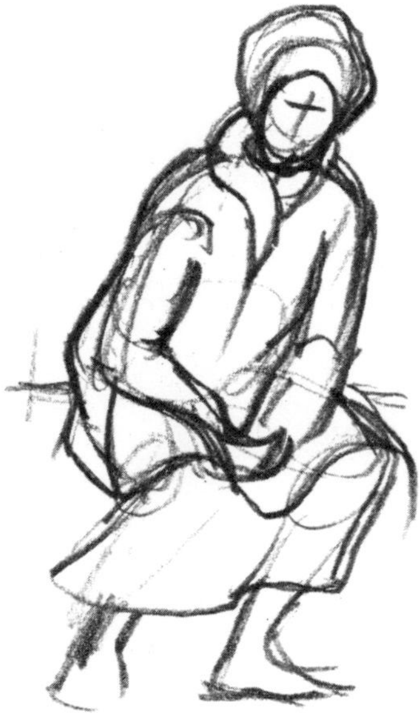

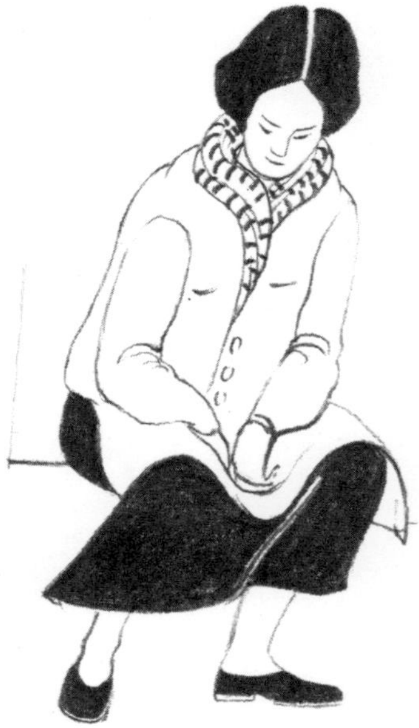

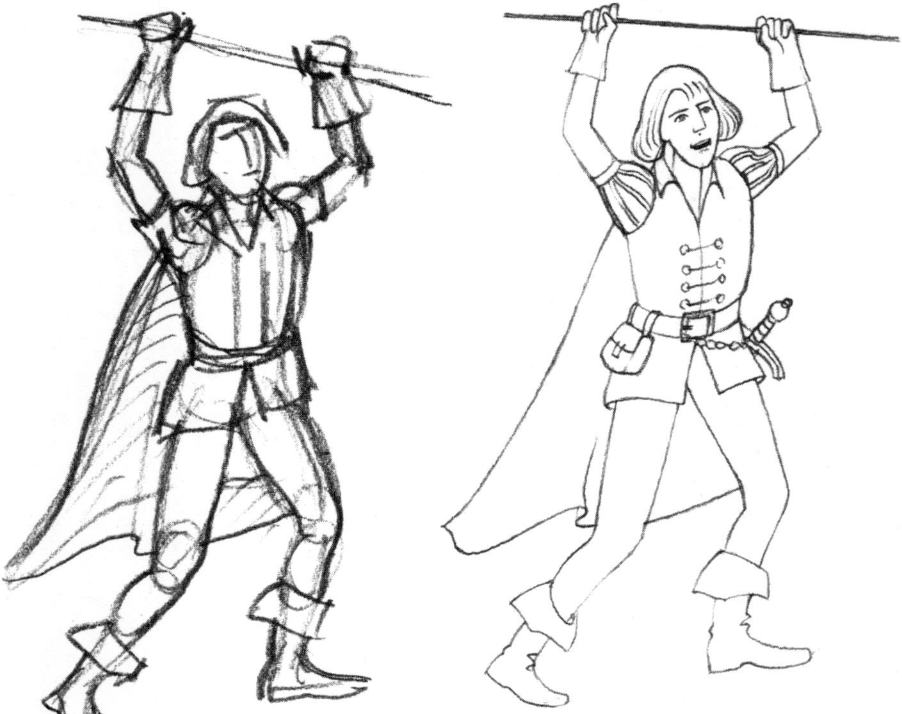

People from earlier times are recognisable by their clothing.

Try to capture this great variety on paper.

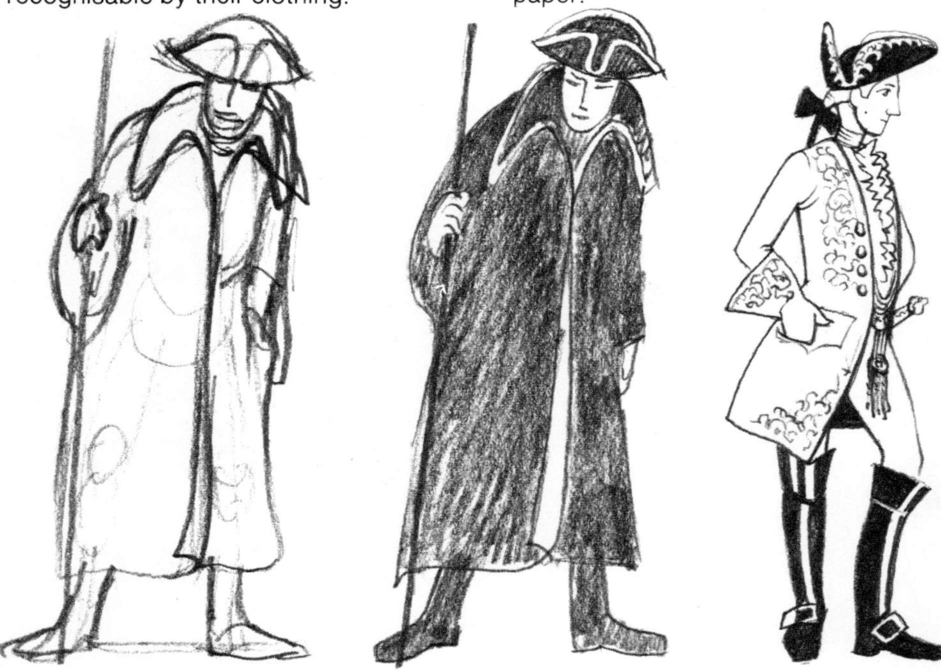

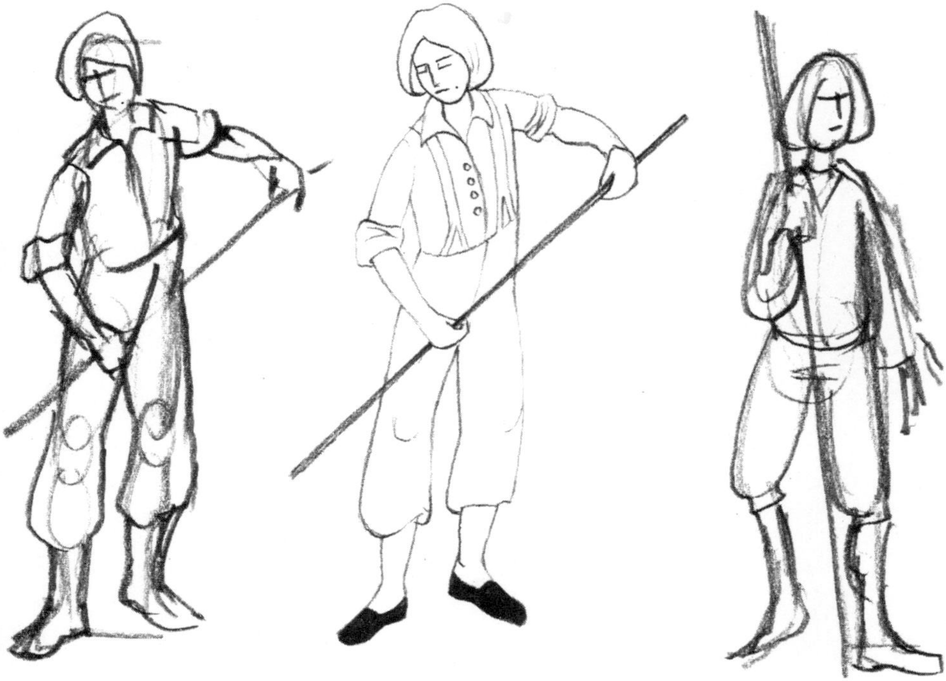

People of the present day in various positions.

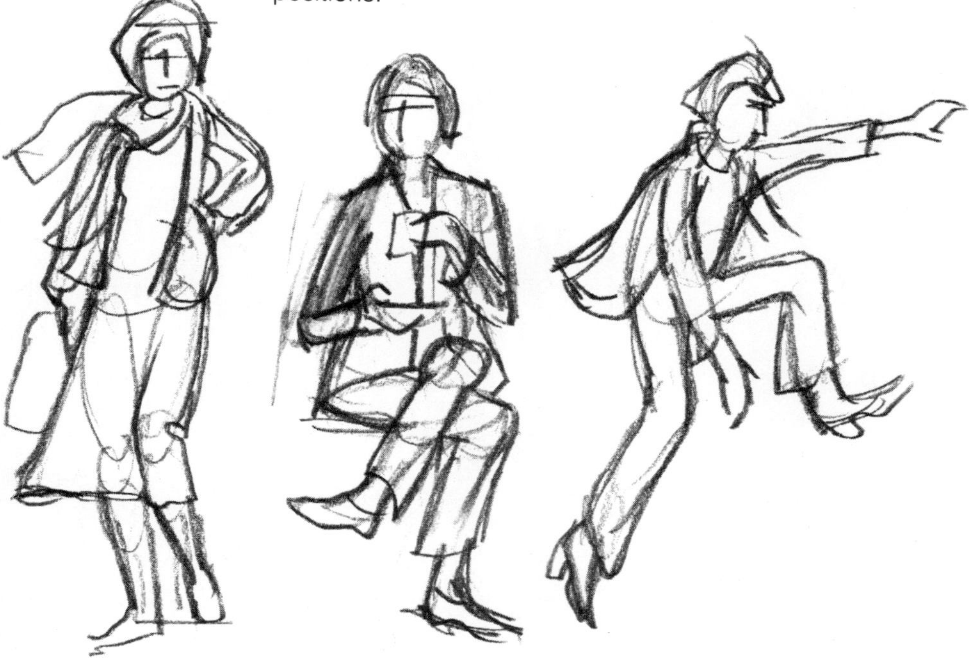

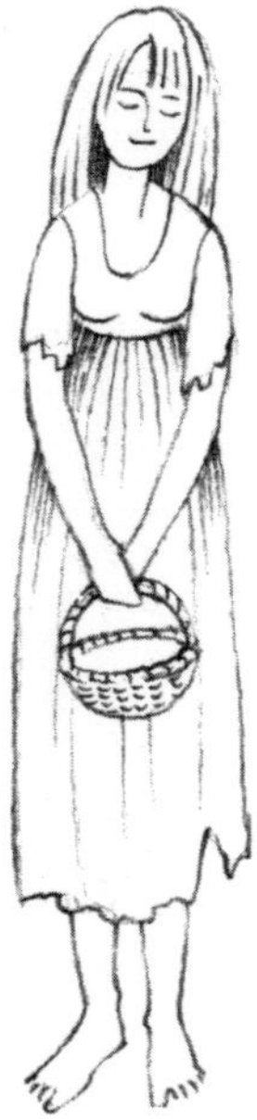

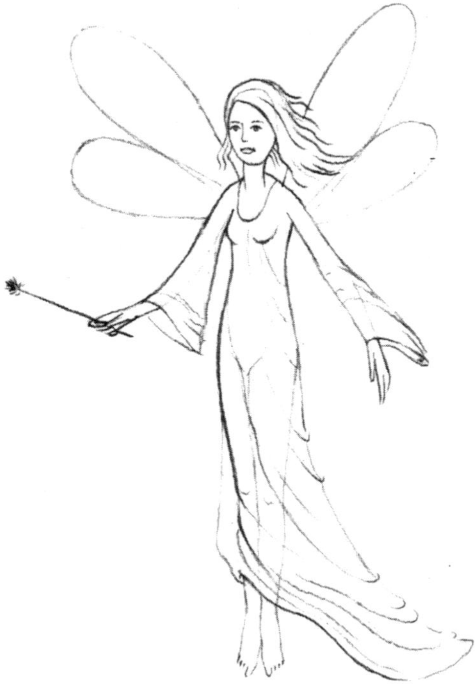

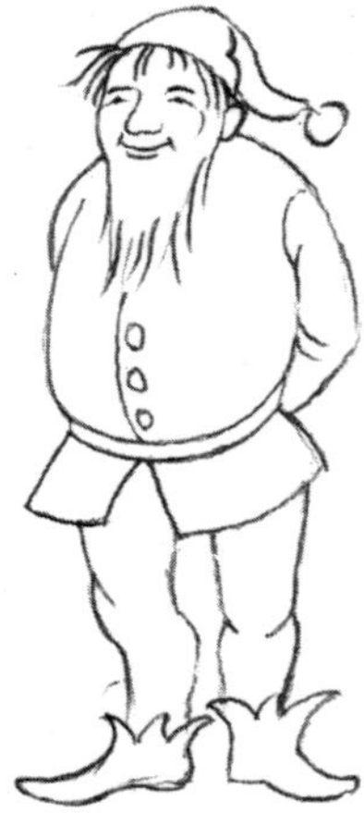

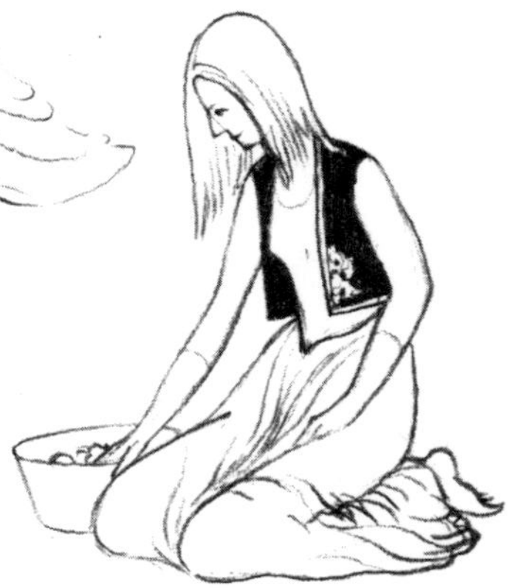

These are all well-known characters from fairy-tales and adventure stories.

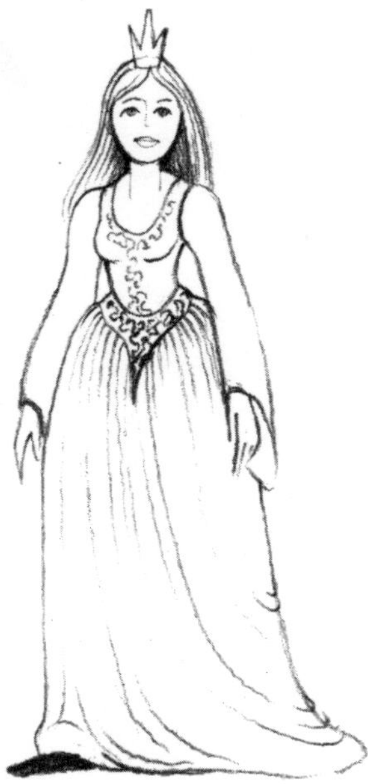

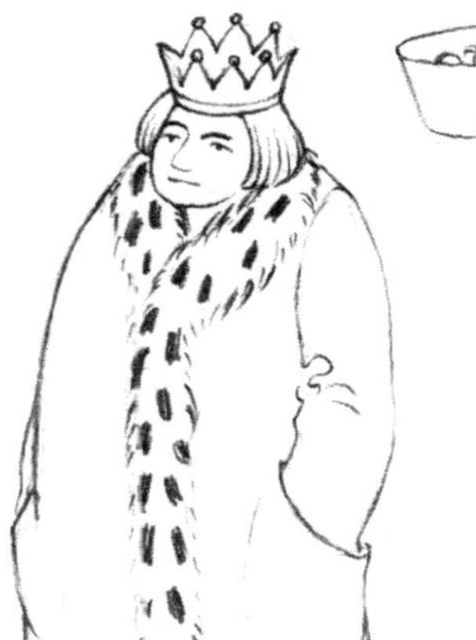

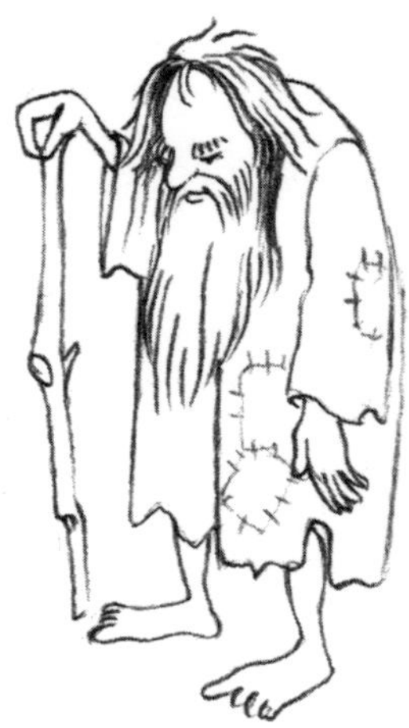

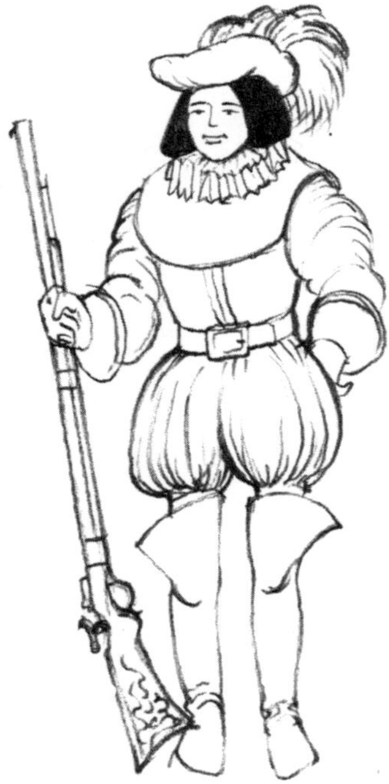

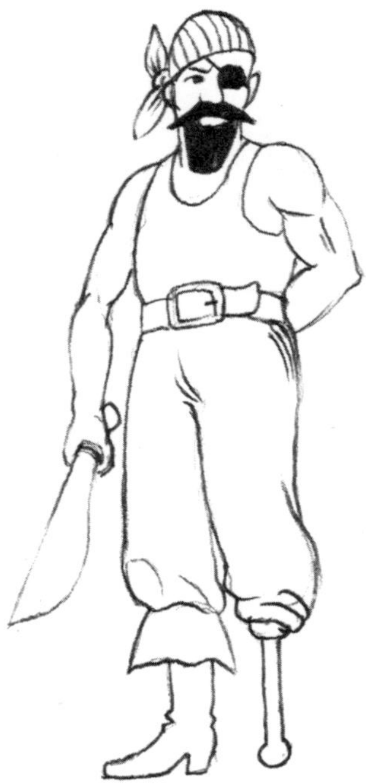

Their clothes and movements provide good opportunities for observation and drawing practice.

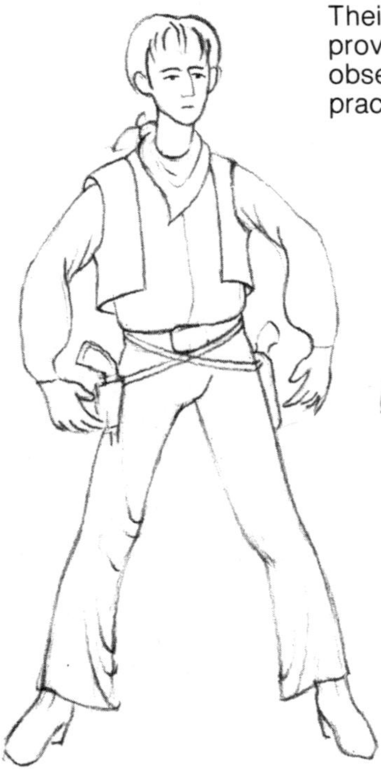

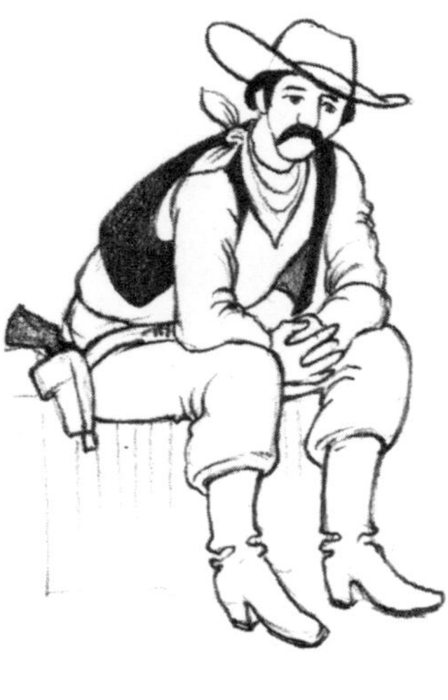

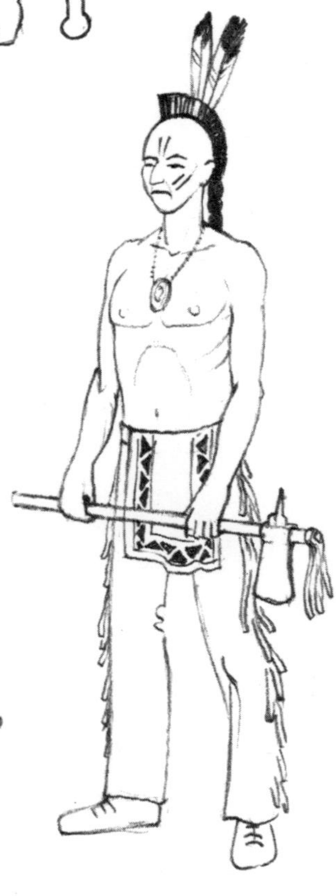

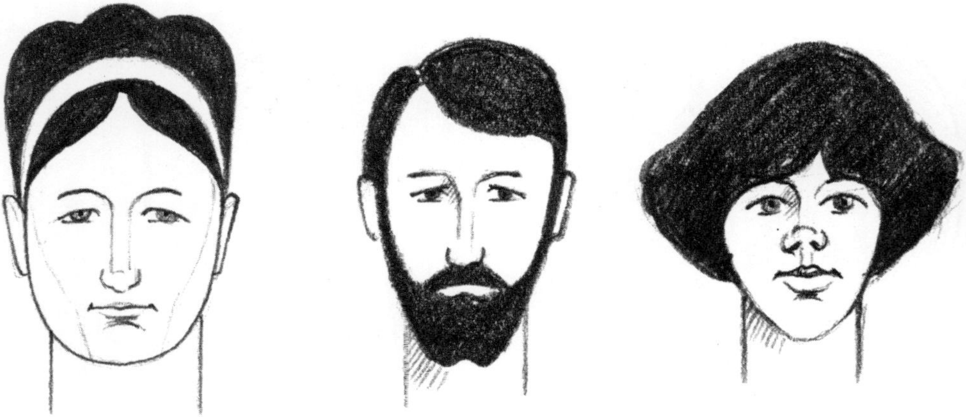

Now try drawing various facial features. This can be done very easily by changing the expressions. Hair, beards and hats are further distinguishing features. All the drawings are two-dimensional.

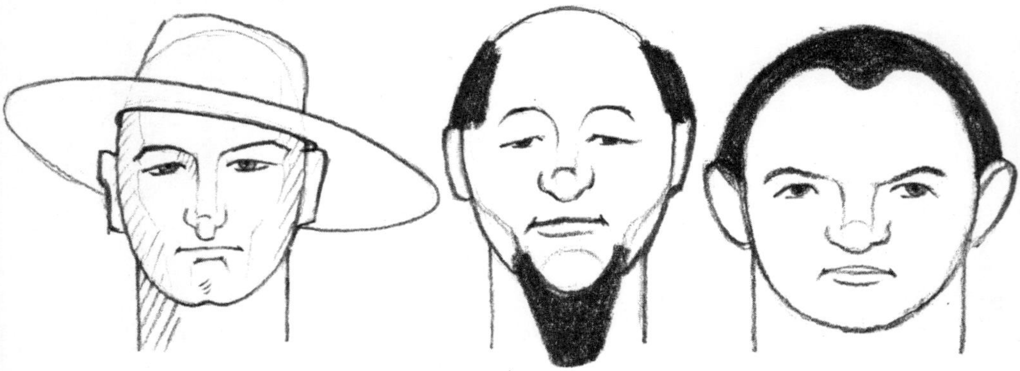

What about faces that express a particular mood?

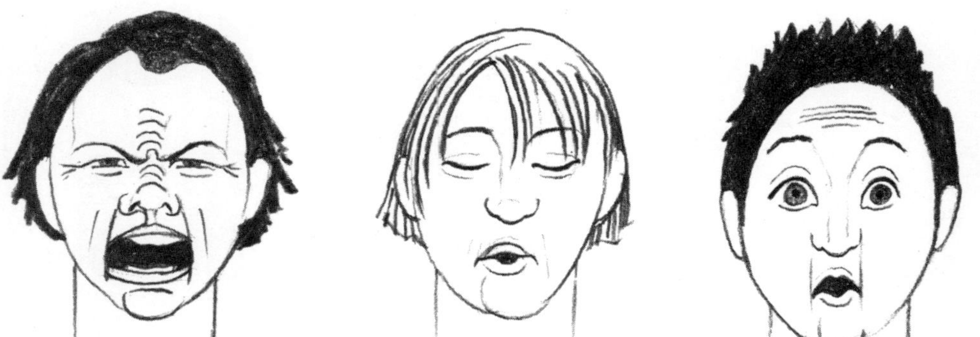

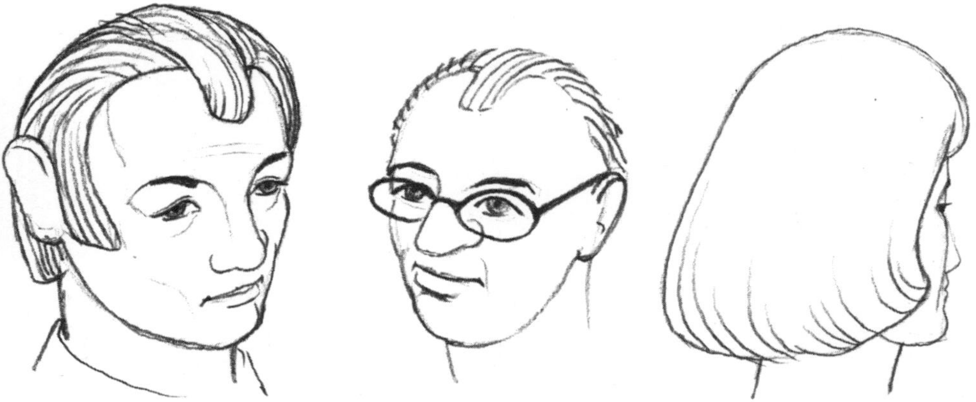

The head in three dimensions.

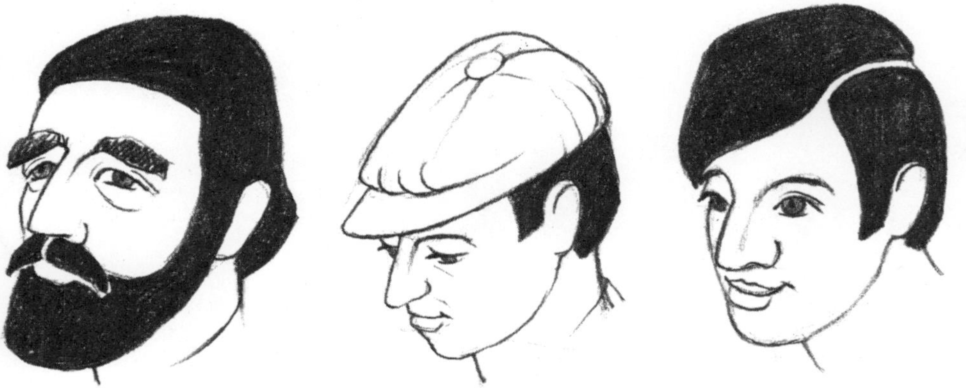

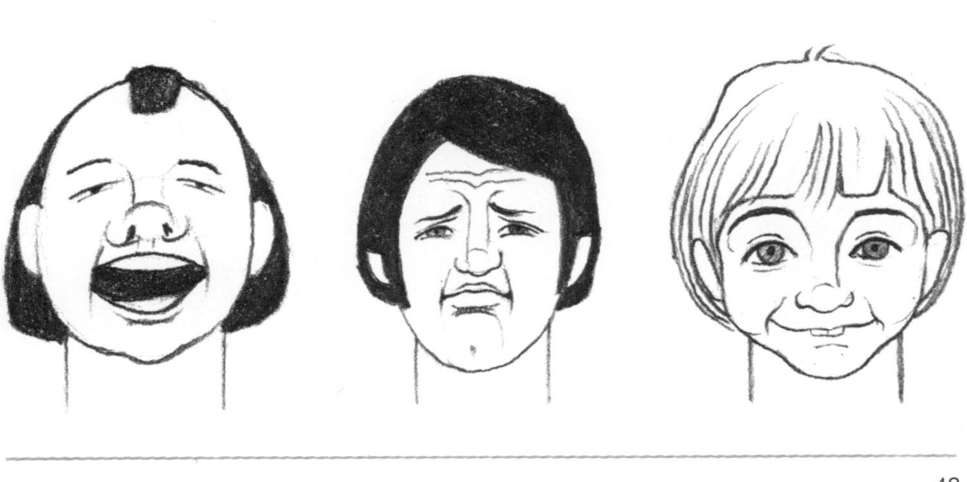

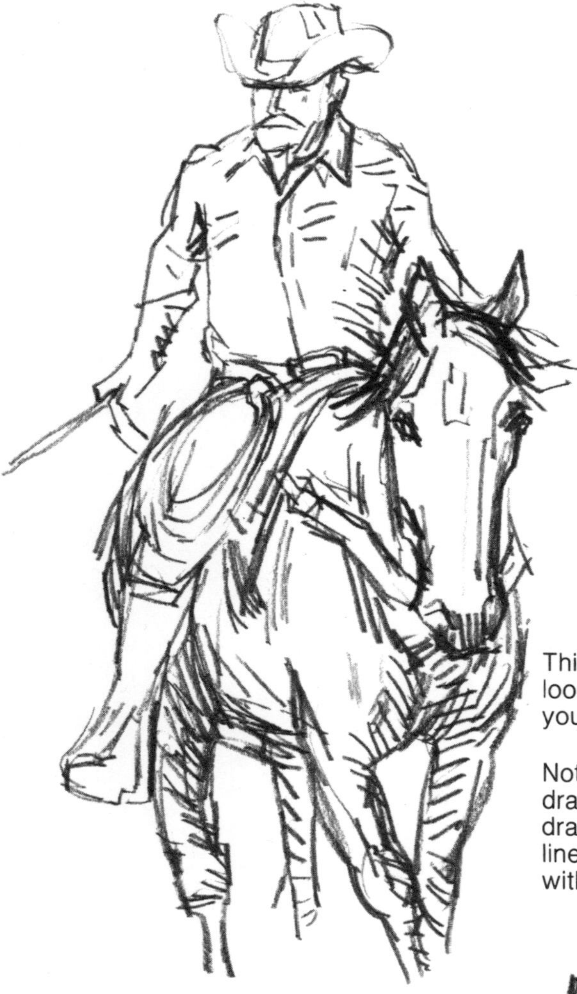

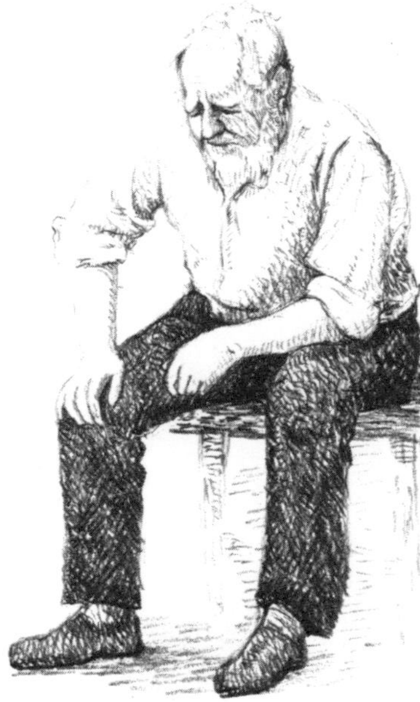

This is what completed drawings can look like. Once you have got this far, you will really start enjoying yourself.

Notice that, in comparison to the drawings on pages 40 and 41, these drawings are made up of many small lines, whereas the others are done with single, clear lines.

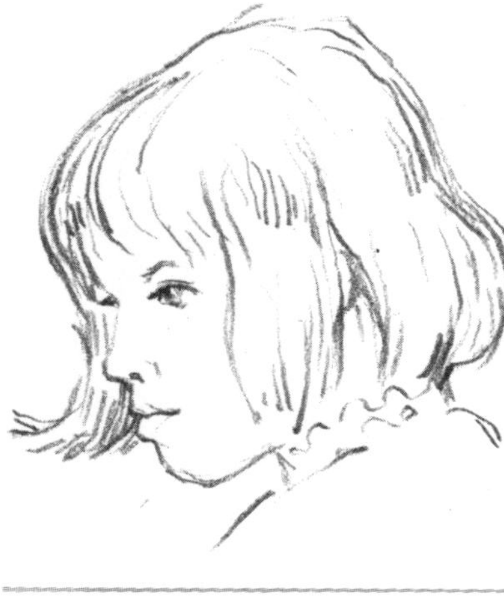

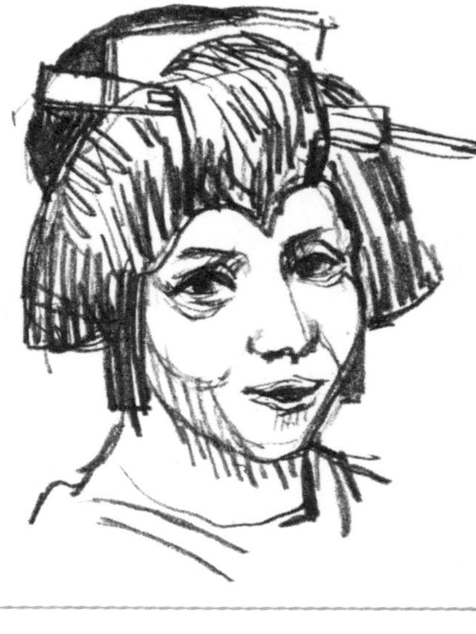

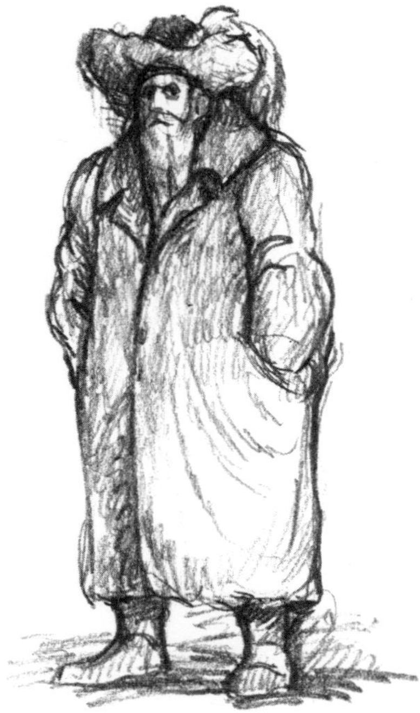

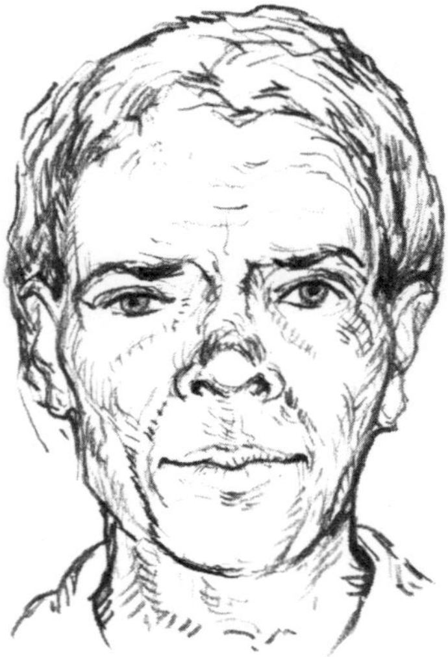

It is obvious that these drawings are more life-like and effective.

Here are some examples from an artist's sketchbook. He has mastered the basic structure and so can abandon it and draw freely.

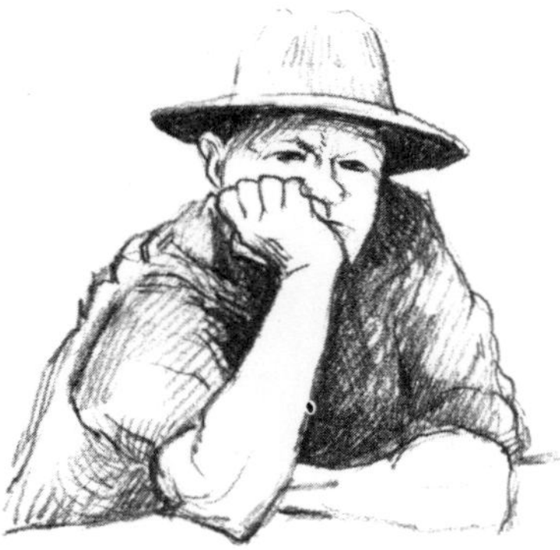

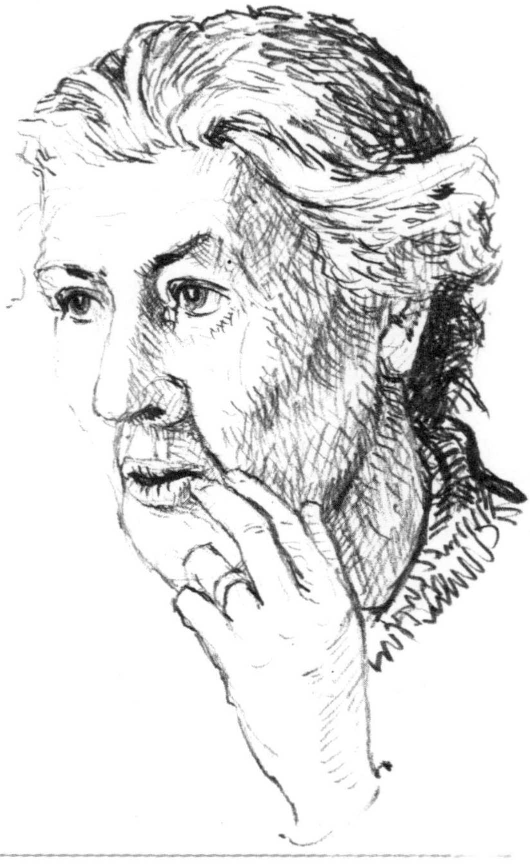

Conclusion

This method of simplification and break-down will teach you to draw properly and freely.

Irrespective of how modest your work is, your own pictures can only be created by drawing freely. The remaining volumes of this series will concentrate on other aspects of the visible world and will approach them using the same method.